Psychotherapy
and the
Lonely Patient

Psychotherapy
and the
Lonely Patient

Samuel M. Natale, Editor

The Psychotherapy Patient Series
E. Mark Stern, Editor

The Haworth Press
New York • London

Psychotherapy and the Lonely Patient has also been published as *The Psychotherapy Patient*, Volume 2, Number 3, Spring 1986.

The Haworth Press, Inc. 12 West 32 Street, New York, NY 10001
EUROSPAN/ Haworth; 3 Henrietta Street, London WC2E 8LU England

Library of Congress Cataloging in Publication Data

Psychotherapy and the lonely patient.

   (The Psychotherapy patient series)
   Includes bibliographies.
   1. Loneliness. 2. Psychotherapy. I. Natale, Samuel M. II. Series.
RC 455.4.L64P79   1986   616.85'2   86-12108
ISBN 0-86656-517-5

Psychotherapy and the Lonely Patient

The Psychotherapy Patient
Volume 2, Number 3

CONTENTS

Loneliness and the Fuller Vision: A Preface   1
    E. Mark Stern

Interrelationships Between Religiousness and Loneliness   3
    Raymond F. Paloutzian
    Aris S. Janigian

  Claims and Issues   4
  Religiousness and Loneliness   6
  Some Processes Which Relate Religiousness and
    Loneliness   9
  Implications   12

Treating Loneliness in Children   15
    Angelo S. Bolea

  Learning Disability Loneliness   16
  Silent Loneliness   18
  Research Method   18
  Testing Instrument   19
  Hypotheses   19
  Techniques for Treating Learning Disability Loneliness   20
  Techniques for Treating Silent Loneliness   22
  Significant Others in Treatment   23
  Conclusion   24

**Loneliness and the Single, the Widowed, and the
  Divorced**   29
    Carole A. Rayburn

  Some Definitions of "Loneliness"   29
  Some Attributes of the Lonely   30
  Gender Differences in Loneliness   31
  Loneliness and Marital Status   34
  Psychotherapy With the Lonely   41

Cognitive Pastoral Psychotherapy With Religious Persons Experiencing Loneliness   47
    Richard D. Parsons
    Robert J. Wicks

Loneliness and the Christian Culture   48
Interventions—A Cognitive Pastoral Focus   51
Intervention—Process   52
Summary   58

Will You Be My Friend? Group Psychotherapy With Lonely People   61
    Brian D. Dufton

Group Psychotherapy   62
Relationship Development   63
Concluding Comments   74

Loneliness and the Aging Client: Psychotherapeutic Considerations   77
    Samuel M. Natale

Experience of Loneliness and Old Age   77

Replication of the Phenomenology of Loneliness in the Therapeutic Dyad   95
    Douglas L. Gerardi

The Therapeutic Setting: The Therapist Communicates With the Patient   95
The Therapist's Contribution to the Patient's Phenomenology of Loneliness   97

A Model for Working With Lonely Clients: Sadler Revisited   109
    Lee J. Richmond
    Edith D. Picken

Loneliness
and the Fuller Vision:
A Preface

Welcome to these most recent pages of *The Psychotherapy Patient* series. As you discover the several social concepts and clinical approaches to the lonely patient, you will begin to discover how isolation and contact, fragmentation and congruence, suspicions and aspirations to love join forces in highlighting the causes and care of friendless alienation. Certainly no single contributor to this volume would claim a panacea for the essential loneliness of existence. What in the end each claims is a proposal to better assess the possibilities of a fuller human vision.

Loneliness, while a response to the absence of another or of others, is never totally so. In the lonely person, objects, places, and persons exist only as fading echoes of an equally fading self. As the expression of boundary loss, loneliness highlights the experience of not knowing where one is. It's as if one's own frustration equals abandonment while the other person's negligence corresponds to contemptuousness. To be certain, loneliness intensifies with the paucity of family and friends. Nonetheless such privations tend to idealize the "betrayer." Although temporary absences taunt the lonely person, what is often seen as unavailable is often unreal. What results is a secret envy or foiled longing prompting a mode of social poverty that bonds individuals to a sense of despair. Certainly no projection is without its point of reference. But in the case of the lonely person, idealized projections, representative of another's claim to popularity, remain in the forefront. Loneliness, by necessity, feeds on such models.

Individuals who in their desperation seek remediation for their loneliness appear to safeguard their illusions of thwarted entitlement. Substance abuse, promiscuity, and autoeroticism provide some distraction from loneliness but rarely touch on its malignant nature. This mirage of predictability and safety, though offering temporary relief, results in an even greater bondage. From a diagnostic standpoint these people rarely experience loneliness *within* the therapeutic enterprise. For even as psychotherapy offers unconditional acceptance under most conditions, it appears less than successful in preparing the tragically lonely person for a fit entry into the alien community.

The question remains: What better can be done for the lonely person who undertakes psychotherapy? Perhaps the best format for treatment is the reinforcement of self-definition. Beyond such buttressing, what is required is a meaningful shoring up of boundaries.

Frieda Fromm-Reichmann (1959), aware of the need for a self with sensible boundaries, counted on the developing significance of the psychotherapeutic bond to help the individual learn to recognize the underlying meaning of pain in the act of lonely withdrawal. She indicated that only through a thoroughgoing renewal of failed interpersonal relationships could the patient reassess earlier losses and so begin to establish new connections with life. Underlining the necessity of such connections undoubtedly helps reinforce the stability and consequent responsiveness of the self. Once the individual begins to understand that he or she as a defined person has significance, then the authentic challenge of others becomes nonpossessive. At such moments loneliness becomes both the predicament and the answer. Only as the individual "stretches" his or her self-concept, or better stated, allows for a full recognition of inner polarities (Zinker, 1977), can there be room for another to witness or be a companion on the journey. Only after such a beholding of the self takes place do all constituent aspects of the self create a sense of wholeness. Once accomplished, the reality of isolation becomes an opportunity for the emergence of cooperation and friendliness.

In this volume, Guest Editor Samuel Natale has gathered a series of contrasting perspectives and views on the phenomenon of loneliness. Though each chapter addresses itself to psychotherapy of the abandoned and the alone, no one contributor to this volume professes a final "cure" for confirmed loneliness. What matters most is that the psychotherapist is often drawn to the task of assisting others in better defining the challenges of absence, loss, and isolation. The hope is that the immediate pain not become cause for inner annihilation. Much stamina and perseverance on the part of both therapist and patient are essential if the lonely motif is to be pondered. As a many-flavored examination of the lonely patient, this volume seeks to open new vantage points and approaches leading to the fuller view of loneliness and its accompanying biddings.

E. Mark Stern
Editor

REFERENCES

Fromm-Reichmann, F. (1959). *Psychoanalysis and psychotherapy, Selected Papers*, D.M. Bullard & E.V. Weigart (Eds.). Chicago: University of Chicago Press.
Zinker, J. (1977). *Creative process in gestalt therapy.* New York: Vintage Books.

Interrelationships Between Religiousness and Loneliness

Raymond F. Paloutzian
Aris S. Janigian

ABSTRACT. Religiousness and loneliness are both concerned with fundamental aspects of human experience; both cause people to grapple with basic issues. Therefore, one would hypothesize an interrelationship between the two. Their relationship, however, is complex. The effect that religion and loneliness have on each other depends upon the type of religiousness and type of loneliness. Religion is a multidimensional variable composed of a matrix of belief, behavior, and experience dimensions. Important for the present analysis is intrinsic and extrinsic religious orientation. Loneliness is construed as a discrepancy between what one wants and what one gets in interpersonal closeness, at both social and emotional levels. An analysis achieved by crossing religious orientation with type of loneliness yields implications for clinical practice and counseling.

Religiousness and loneliness—both topics of basic concern and intimate experience in human life—are related. But their relationship is not simple or straightforward. To understand the relationship between religiousness and loneliness, and to apply this understanding to clinical and practical work, we must comprehend the multifaceted nature of each: Loneliness as the result of a discrepancy between what one wants and what one gets in social relationships and emotional intimacy; religion as a multidimensional variable composed of an array of beliefs, behaviors, and motives. Like so many social psychological processes, their interrelationship forms an intricate web that affects the quality of life. But it is a web that is rich in meaning. We will see that an analysis of how each one affects the other yields insights of practical use for professionals who see clients who are religious and for whom loneliness is a symptom.

Raymond F. Paloutzian, Ph.D., received his doctorate in Social Psychology from The Claremont Graduate School. He is author of *Invitation to the Psychology of Religion* (Scott, Foreman & Co., 1983), and is Professor of Psychology at Westmont College, Santa Barbara, California.

Aris S. Janigian, M.A., is a doctoral student in social psychology at The Claremont Graduate School.

CLAIMS AND ISSUES

Religion and Loneliness Are Basic and Pervasive

Religiousness and loneliness are two areas of the human experience that are common, and prompt people to raise the basic questions of life. Such questions are often painful to ask, and they elude a simple answer.

The frequency of concern with such issues is illustrated by recent polling data: For example, America has a substantial religiously oriented population in which 94% of the people believe in God, 89% pray, and 84% feel that religion is an important part of their lives (Gallup, 1979-80). Furthermore, millions have turned to traditional religion, and millions of others have turned to cultic religion (Paloutzian, 1983).

Similarly, loneliness appears to be a frequent problem. Projections based on survey data suggest that between 20 and 80 million people are lonely to a painful degree (Peplau & Perlman, 1982; Weiss, 1973).

Because both religiousness and loneliness strike a fundamental (and similar-sounding) chord in human life, and because both are widespread, we are prompted to ask questions about their possible interrelationship. In other words, religion deals with basic issues and is intensely personal for many, and loneliness is also an intensely personal experience. Therefore, it is reasonable for us to ask whether and how these may interact in people's lives. The answers, we hope, yield information and ideas useful in psychotherapy and counseling.

Case Studies

Contemporary case studies illustrate some of the ways that an association between religiousness and degree of loneliness occurs. Consider the following true accounts of religious behavior, each one involving the persons's degree of loneliness in some way:

1. A young man feels lonely and unloved, and lacks a sense of belonging. He begins participating in religious activities at his church, contributing his skills to group activities. He becomes a member of the church, feels that he is now where he belongs, and his loneliness declines.
2. A man in his early 20s has a religious experience in which he claims he feels a "oneness with God." As a consequence, he becomes a social isolate, living alone, and tries to re-create that experience.
3. A couple who live in a small farm town were raised participating in their local denominational church. After their marriage, they still at-

tend the same church, participate in its activities, and have the same close church ties they always had. They have never felt lonely to a serious degree.

4. A person joins a religious cult, out of a desire for simple friendship (Cox, 1977).
5. A woman believes that by praying she is talking with a personal God whose spirit resides inside her. She says that such conversation with a personal God accomplishes many things, including helping her not to feel so existentially lonely.
6. Because of his religious beliefs, a young man decides to work actively for a social cause. He gives much time and energy toward this. As a consequence, he feels a great sense of purpose in life, is distracted from self-absorbing introspection, and no longer feels the loneliness that he felt before.

The above accounts point out not only the power of religious belief to motivate behavior and affect feelings, but also illustrate some of the ways that religious belief or behavior and the desire for closeness and belonging affect each other and loneliness. For example, cases #1 and #4 illustrate the treatment hypothesis—the idea that religious activities reduce loneliness. Case #2 suggests a different idea—that a religious experience can lead one to become an isolate. Case #3 is a prototype of the deterrence hypothesis. In this case, severe degree of loneliness never occurred because the people had always been in their primary religious network. In case #5, it is the "personalness" of the content of the religious belief (trust in a personal God), coupled with the performance of a religious practice (prayer) which the actor believes is communication with God, that affects loneliness. In case #6, loneliness is reduced by distraction of the actor's attention from himself by providing him with task orientation—a purpose in life.

If loneliness and religiousness are associated in ways illustrated by the above cases, it may be because both touch upon fundamental aspects of human experience and the quality of life, and because both are so widespread.

Considerations for Practice

Several kinds of claims are made about how religion and loneliness are related. Some of these were illustrated above. One highly popular claim today is that participating in religion can help you not be lonely. On the other hand, some of the world's most influential religious leaders suffered intense and painful loneliness. Some people use a religious practice, such

as prayer or Bible reading, as a coping mechanism for loneliness (Paloutzian & Ellison, 1982). Others suggest that religious aloneness (such as
might be attained by isolation or meditation) makes them not feel lonely
because it helps them feel at one with a personal God (Suedfeld, 1982).
Finally, some propose that participating in religious social activities promotes the behavior of sharing and caring, and that a sense of belonging
and of actually being needed is simply a natural by-product.

Therefore, though the exact degree of interdependence between religiousness and loneliness is unclear, it is at least clear that for certain kinds
of religious clients we should expect their religious beliefs and practices
to affect and be affected by how lonely they feel.

The outcome of our considerations should be some possible strategies
for the therapist for strongly religious patients. The therapist can exploit
the entanglement of central religious beliefs with symptom difficulties
like loneliness. That is, the patient's religion can serve either as an anchor
that the therapist can draw upon as a source of strength for the patient, or
as a target toward which the therapist can aim the patient as he or she
moves the patient from peripheral toward central facets of his or her disturbance.

Similarly, our understanding of the relation between religiousness and
loneliness can help us in making decisions about such things as whether
clinician or counselor should hold the same religious beliefs as the client;
whether such beliefs should be made public in advertisment and/or in in-
take interviews; when the therapist should encourage or discourage
religious participation; or whether the therapist should view a client's
religion as a deterrent to or a treatment of loneliness.

RELIGIOUSNESS AND LONELINESS

Because the above remarks are stated in general terms, they do not
yield very precise understanding about whether religiousness and loneliness actually are related, or if so, by what process. In order to help us
understand just how religiousness and loneliness are related, therefore,
we must identify the key components of each construct. We will then be
in a better position to understand the process by which religiousness and
loneliness affect each other and contribute to the client's level of well-
being.

Religiousness

The key distinctions we need to keep in mind about religiousness for
our purposes are that it exists as both a matter of personal commitment
and as an arena in which social-psychological processes operate; that it is

composed of several dimensions of belief, behavior, and feelings; and that it can be more or less central (i.e., instrinsic or extrinsic) in a person's life. Religion is multidimensional, not a single attribute that some people have and others do not have. Though the intricacies of this multidimensionality are beyond the scope of this paper (for detailed treatment, see Batson & Ventis, 1982; Meadow & Kahoe, 1984; Paloutzian, 1983; Spilka, Hood, & Gorsuch, 1985), keeping in mind the above distinctions will help us understand how religiousness and loneliness interact.

The centrality of a person's religion is evidenced by the degree to which it is intrinsic or extrinsic. Intrinsic religion is said to function as a "master motive" (Allport, 1950, 1966) which serves to guide other attitudes, feelings, and actions. The intrinsically religious person, having internalized the belief into the personality, is said to "live" the faith. Hence, religious behavior is an expression of an internal motive.

In contrast, extrinsic religion is that which is motivated by some other nonreligious end. The extrinsically religious person claims belief or displays religious practice for utilitarian personal or social benefit. Hence it is said that the extrinsic "uses" the faith.

(Scales to measure whether people are high or low on intrinsicness and extrinsicness exist [Robinson & Shaver, 1973]. Thus, it is possible to order people along a scale of the degree to which they hold centralized, internalized religious faith.)

Loneliness

A Discrepancy Between What One Wants and What One Gets

Loneliness is not just a feeling of being alone. Neither is it merely an attribute, as if to say that "Patient Jones is a lonely person by nature of his or her personality." Loneliness is not a personality trait (though there are traits that moderate it). Rather, loneliness is an aversive feeling that occurs when people do not get what they want, need, or expect in interpersonal closeness. It is what happens in this social dimension, interacting with the person's needs, expectancies and personality, that determines loneliness. Hence,

> loneliness is the unpleasant experience that occurs when a person's network of social relationships is significantly deficient in either quality or quantity. This definition shares three points of agreement with the way most other scholars view loneliness. First, loneliness results from a deficiency in a person's social relationships. Loneliness occurs when there is a mismatch between a person's actual

social relations and the person's needs or desires for social contact . . . . Second, loneliness is a subjective experience; it is not synonymous with objective social isolation. People can be alone without being lonely, or lonely in a crowd. Third, the experience of loneliness is aversive. Although loneliness may be a spur to personal growth, the experience itself is unpleasant and distressing. (Perlman & Peplau, 1984)

Implicit in this view is the idea that it is not a person's absolute level of attained quality or quantity of social contact that determines the degree of loneliness. Rather, it is the person's attained level, relative to desired and expected level. People who want a lot of interpersonal closeness, and get it, are not lonely. People who want only a little, and get it, are not lonely. But people who get less than they want or expect feel lonely to that degree.

The above conceptual model of loneliness is complemented by an empirical definition of what the lonely experience is actually like. Research strategies include attempts to cluster the major components of loneliness into sets of attributes (Horowitz, French, & Anderson, 1982) and generating lists of adjectives that people say are part of their lonely experience (Paloutzian & Ellison, 1982; Rubenstein & Shaver, 1982). In general, these findings reveal that lonely people think that they "Don't fit in," that they are not wanted by the people or groups that they value belonging to, that they feel emotionally unsatisfied in their relationships with others, and that they feel a lack of understanding with the people closest to them.

(An abbreviated Loneliness Scale that could have applications for clinical or counseling sessions where a short index is needed has been developed, based on such findings. See Table 1. For more precise testing, we recommend the 20-item revised UCLA Loneliness Scale [Russell, Peplau, & Cutrona, 1980].)

Social and Emotional Loneliness

Weiss (1973) hypothesizes that there are two distinct types of loneliness, each based on a different type of discrepancy. Social loneliness results from the deficiency of friends and cohorts in a milieu. Emotional loneliness results from the lack of a bond with an intimate, primary other. Weiss also suggests that each type of lack results in different types of distress. This distinction has recently received empirical support (Russell, Cutrona, Rose, & Yurko, 1984). Practitioners should be sensitive to these two different types of loneliness, especially as they manifest themselves in religious people.

Table 1

Abbreviated Loneliness Scale (ABLS)[a]

Please circle the choice that best indicates how often each of the following statements describes you in general;

   O = Often   S = Sometimes   R = Rarely   N = Never

1. I feel like the people most important to me understand me.   O S R N

2. I feel lonely.   O S R N

3. I feel like I am wanted by the people/groups I value belonging to. O S R N

4. I feel emotionally distant from people in general.   O S R N

5. I have as many close relationships as I want.   O S R N

6. I have felt lonely during my life.   O S R N

7. I feel emotionally satisfied in my relationship with people.   O S R N

Copyright (c) 1982 by Raymond F. Paloutzian and Craig W. Ellison.

[a] Items are scored 1 to 4 so that a higher number reflects greater loneliness. Odd-numbered items are positively worded. Reverse scoring for these items. The ABLS score is the sum of the seven responses. For more information see Paloutzian & Ellison (1982).

SOME PROCESSES WHICH RELATE RELIGIOUSNESS AND LONELINESS

Though the above is but a single sketch of the complexity and intricacies of religious orientation and loneliness, it is sufficient to allow us to explore some of the common processes that affect them. We can identify two types of effects, both of which are results of basic psychological processes. In one case, psychological factors operate to produce effects not likely found elsewhere—because of the unique way that religion may function in the person's life (e.g., the psychological effects of belief in an absolute or personal God). In the second case, psychological factors which are common to religion as well as to other areas of life (e.g., group processes) operate to produce effects similar to those found in the other areas. Additional mediating processes may be involved in either case. Examining two types of religious orientation crossed with two types of loneliness illustrates how some of these processes work.

Religious Orientation × Loneliness

Social Loneliness

Personal religious belief generally involves strong convictions about the nature of God, people's relationship to God, and the implications these beliefs have for people's interaction with each other. These concerns are central to human behavior and affect. A social system like a church or synagogue often provides an environment to openly express and share such beliefs. It would be fair to say, therefore, that one's religion would be rich if practiced and experienced in a community.

Recent research illustrates some of the social psychological processes that would operate in such a religious group to lower loneliness. For example, we know that denser social networks (Stokes, 1985) and self-disclosure (Franzoi & Davis, 1985), especially to peers (Solano, Batten, & Parish, 1982), are associated with lower loneliness. Importantly, the more meaningful people's interaction with each other is, the less lonely they feel (Wheeler, Reis, & Nezlek, 1983). Because participating in a religious group places one in a social network that often encourages meaningful self-disclosures to peers, it is easy to see how such groups set the stage for exchanging intimacies, reducing barriers, developing interpersonal trust and a sense of belonging, and adjusting expected and desired degrees of interaction, all of which would lessen loneliness.

The opposite effects would be expected of a community of worship that was not congenial nor encouraging of one's particular mode of religious practice and belief. The plethora of denominations or sects within single religions, and their variation in forms of worship, is an indicator of the variety of settings needed to accommodate individual religious styles. The absence of a healthy, accepting environment for religious expression may lead one to feel frustrated, confused, and socially lonely.

How a person responds to social loneliness resulting from a feeling of alienation from a religious community may have different effects, depending upon the person's religious orientation. An extrinsically religious person who has primarily associated God with the group may cope with his or her loneliness by turning away from religion altogether. No longer able to accept the norms and function of the group, he or she can no longer accept God or religion. On the other hand, an intrinsically religious person whose faith is the "master motive" in life may retain a belief in God, but leave that church and find a more congenial religious community.

Emotional Loneliness

As discussed earlier, emotional loneliness is a symptom of the lack of an intimate bond with a primary other. Though this bond is conceptualized as existing between people, in the case of a religious person it may also exist in relation to God. Many religious people, particularly those in the Judeo-Christian heritage, describe their relationship to God as personal and intimate. This is evident in religious colloquialisms (e.g., "Jesus is my best friend"; "I committed myself to God") or in the sacred writings of these religions (e.g., "Come let us reason together"; "God turned his back from his people"). The adherence to religious practices such as prayer and devotions are often seen as determining the wholesomeness of one's relationship to God. Likewise, for many religious people, behaviors or thoughts which counter their perception of God's will may evoke feelings of alienation from God. The consequence for intrinsically religious people who perceive God as deeply personal may be emotional loneliness.

We would speculate that such emotional loneliness is less likely to be a problem for extrinsically religious persons. This is because for them, an apparent lesser degree of personal commitment permits behaviors and thoughts incongruent with the religious teaching, with less likelihood of feelings of alienation from God.

Purpose in Life

Recent research indicates additional factors which are involved in the relation between religiousness and loneliness. Most important is purpose in life. It has been shown that high scores on the Purpose in Life Test (Crumbaugh & Maholick, 1969), designed to measure sense of meaning in life as construed by Frankl (1963), are correlated with intrinsic religious orientation (Paloutzian & Ellison, 1982; Paloutzian, Jackson, & Crandall, 1978; Soderstrom & Wright, 1977) and with lower loneliness (Dufton, 1984). It has also been found that people who believe that their lives have meaning and direction—not necessarily religious—are less likely to be lonely (Rubenstein & Shaver, 1980). There was not an overall relation between belief and loneliness. Thus, it is easy to conceptualize how intrinsic religious orientation leads to a sense of purpose, which focuses one's attention off of a self-absorbing concern with one's own feelings, and as a consequence lowers loneliness.

The above analysis is only illustrative, but it does indicate the types of social psychological processes that would operate through religious beliefs and/or practices to have some affect in deterring or reducing loneliness. In all cases, "interaction" seems to be the catchword. Religious people's likelihood of suffering from loneliness, and their response to it, depend upon their religious orientation and type of loneliness.

IMPLICATIONS

Practice

Some practical suggestions can be drawn from the above analysis of religiousness and loneliness. But first, we are not saying that clinicians and counselors should promote religiousness in their clients. We are saying, however, that for those clients who happen to be religious, the therapist or counselor can draw upon the client's belief and group affiliation as a resource that can be exploited for therapeutic purposes. For example, taking emotional loneliness as a cue, the therapist may probe the structure of the client's relationship to God or religion. This practice may aid therapists in alleviating the client's symptoms of loneliness and perhaps lead the client to develop a more fruitful religious life.

We would suggest that the therapeutic approach for a person suffering from social loneliness precipitated by change in the person's need for the religious community, or the nature of the community, should be different for extrinsic and intrinsic persons. For an intrinsic person, therapy may include encouraging the person to explore different congregations to better meet his or her religious needs. For an extrinsic person, the therapist may want to redirect the person's orientation, and help him or her develop a deeper commitment. Scales of religious orientation are available which can help the therapist assess the orientation of the client (Robinson & Shaver, 1973; Batson & Ventis, 1982; Spilka, Hood, & Gorsuch, 1985).

For therapists to gain skill at exploiting the potential therapeutic benefits of a client's religiousness, however, there are some prerequisites.

1. The therapist needs to know the religious belief system and practices of clients sufficiently well to be able to dialogue with them effectively, to understand and appreciate their role in the client's life, and know how to draw upon them. This requires "theological realism" (Bergin, 1980).
2. Therapists needs to be able to identify different religious orientations and different forms of loneliness, and be able to exploit their interaction for benefit in treatment.
3. Clinicians are free to accept the limits of their own knowledge of clients' beliefs, and consequently are free to refer the client to an appropriate professional.

4. The importance of the therapist's beliefs is almost as important as those of the client. This is true in two respects: First, the therapist's beliefs can influence how he or she handles the client in light of his or her own beliefs; second, whether or not the beliefs of the therapist and client correspond can affect whether the therapist is believable to the client. Believability is prerequisite to effective treatment.

Loneliness as a Symptom

Finally,this analysis of the processes that interrelate loneliness and re-ligiousness suggests that loneliness per se is not likely to be the client's real problem. Nowhere have we suggested that loneliness is an attribute or trait. Rather, loneliness is best seen as a symptom of unmet desires or expectancies for interpersonal relationships. As such, it could be a side effect or symptom of personality traits that would lead one to have unreal-istically high expectations for social contact or emotional closeness with respect to their congregation or God. As related to religious variables, degree of loneliness would seem to be a function of the degree to which the person's constellation of beliefs, practices, and intrinsic or extrinsic orientation fosters a sense of purpose and belonging. High levels of loneliness would indicate that such needs were not being met. Hence, the religious context could be drawn upon to meet them by lowering expec-tancies and raising attained levels of interpersonal closeness.

REFERENCES

Allport, G.W. (1950). *The Individual and his religion.* New York: Macmillan.
Allport, G.W. (1966). The religious context of prejudice. *Journal for the Scientific Study of Religion, 5*, 447-457.
Batson, C.D. & Ventis, W.L. (1982). *The religious experience: A social-psychological perspective.* New York: Oxford University Press.
Bergin, A.E. (1980). Psychotherapy and religious values. *Journal of Consulting and Clinical Psychology, 48*, 95-105.
Cox. H. (1977). *Turning East: The promise and peril of the new Orientalism.* New York: Simon and Schuster.
Crumbaugh, J.C. & Maholick, L.T. (1969). *The purpose in life test.* Munster, IN: Psychometric Affiliates.
Dufton, B. (1984). *Inter-relationships between loneliness and religiosity.* Unpublished doctoral dissertation, University of Manitoba, Winnipeg, Manitoba, Canada.
Frankl, V. (1963). *Man's search for meaning.* New York: Washington Square Press.
Franzoi, S.L. Davis, M.H. (1985). Adolescent self-disclosure and loneliness: Private self-con-sciousness and parental influences. *Journal of Personality and Social Psychology, 48*, 768-780.
Gallup Opinion Index. (1979-80). *Religion in America.* Princeton, NJ: The American Institute of Public Opinion.
Horowitz, L.M., French, R., & Anderson, C.A. (1982.) The prototype of a lonely person. In L.A. Peplau & D. Perlman (Eds.), *Loneliness: A sourcebook of current theory, research and therapy* (pp. 183-205). New York: Wiley-Interscience.

Meadow, M.J. & Kahoe, R.D. (1984). *Psychology of religion: Religion in individual lives.* New York: Harper & Row.

Paloutzian, R.F. (1983). *Invitation to the psychology of religion.* Glenview, IL: Scott, Foresman & Co.

Palotuzian, R.F. & Ellison, C.W. (1982). Loneliness, spiritual well-being, and the quality of life. In L.A. Peplau & D. Perlman (Eds.), *Loneliness: A sourcebook of current theory, research and therapy.* (pp. 237-244). New York: Wiley-Interscience.

Paloutzian, R.F., Jackson, S.L. & Crandall, J.E. (1978). Conversion experience, belief system, and personal and ethical attitudes. *Journal of Psychology and Theology, 6,* 266-275.

Peplau, L.A. & Perlman, D., (Eds.) (1982). *Loneliness: A sourcebook of current theory, research and therapy.* New York: Wiley-Interscience.

Perlman, D. & Peplau, L.A. (1984). Loneliness research: A survey of empirical findings. In L.A. Peplau & S.E. Goldston (Eds.), *Preventing the harmful consequences of severe and persistent loneliness* (DHHS Publication No. ADM 84-1312). Washington, DC: U.S. Government Printing Office.

Robinson, J.P. & Shaver, P.R. (Eds.) (1973). *Measure of social psychological attitudes.* Ann Arbor, MI: Institute for Social Research.

Rubenstein, C.M. & Shaver, P. (1980). Loneliness in two northeastern cities. In J. Hartog, J.R. Andy, & Y. Cohen (Eds.), *The anatomy of loneliness* (pp. 319-337). New York: International Universities Press.

Rubenstein, C.M. & Shaver, P. (1982). The experience of loneliness. In L.A. Peplau & D. Perlman (Eds.), *Loneliness: A sourcebook of current theory, research and therapy (pp. 206-223).* New York: Wiley-Interscience.

Russell, D., Peplau, L.A., & Cutrona, C.E. (1980). The revised UCLA loneliness scale: Concurrent and discriminant validity evidence. *Journal of Personality and Social Psychology, 39,* 472-480.

Russell, D., Cutrona, C.E., Rose, J., & Yurko, K. (1984). Social and emotional loneliness: An examination of Weiss' typology of loneliness. *Journal of Personality and Social Psychology, 46,* 1313-1321.

Soderstrom, D. & Wright, W.E. (1977). Religious orientation and meaning in life. *Journal of Clinical Psychology, 33,* 65-68.

Solano, C.H., Batten, P.G., & Parish, E.A. (1982). Loneliness and patterns of self-disclosure. *Journal of Personality and Social Psychology, 43,* 524-531.

Spilka, B., Hood, R.W., & Gorsuch, R.L. (1985). *The psychology of religion: An empirical approach.* Englewood Cliffs, NJ: Prentice-Hall.

Stokes, J.P. (1985). The relation of social network and individual difference variables to loneliness. *Journal of Personality and Social Psychology, 48,* 981-990.

Suedfeld, P. (1982). Aloneness as a healing experience. In L.A. Peplau & D. Perlman (Eds.), *Loneliness: A sourcebook of current theory, research and therapy* (pp. 54-67). New York: Wiley-Interscience.

Weiss, R. (1973). *Loneliness: The experience of emotional and social isolation.* Cambridge, MA: MIT Press.

Wheeler, L., Reis, H., & Nezlek, J. (1983). Loneliness, social interaction, and sex roles. *Journal of Personality and Social Psychology, 45,* 943-953.

Treating Loneliness in Children

Angelo S. Bolea

ABSTRACT. A detailed description of a multisensory approach to treating two major types of loneliness in children is described in this research. Learning disabled children and children who are sexually and physically abused were studied and treated with a neuropsychological emphasis in terms of two types of loneliness; exampled by defensive attitude and a secret or silent type of loneliness. A self-concept measure was employed from which a loneliness score was derived to test two major hypotheses dealing with the ability to differentiate between types of loneliness and the ability to measure changes toward dealing with loneliness.

The research showed that treatment with art therapy coupled with family counseling was effective in surfacing feelings of loneliness and circumventing defenses such as Denial and People Pleasing. The Pictorial Self-Concept measure utilized, avoided the learning disability and was sensitive to changes in willingness to disclose and deal with loneliness.

Loneliness is a human experience which may be viewed as almost universal. It began to appear in psychological literature in the 1950s. However, it was not until the late 1970s and the early 1980s that serious research was done studying loneliness in children. Objectives of this report are two-fold: First, it will identify at least two different types of loneliness experienced by children, namely the Silent Loneliness, and the Learning Disability Loneliness. Secondly, there will be a focus on description of techniques and approaches used in alleviating and preventing loneliness in children.

Loneliness is defined as an unpleasant experience, mood, or feeling that is created by a discrepancy between what a child wished, or expected from a relationship, and what a child actually perceives as experienced in the relationship. It is further accepted that children as well as adults have a natural human need for emotional intimacy in relationships and that when disruption occurs in those relationships, loneliness results (Peplau & Perlman, 1982; Perlman & Peplau, 1981). Therefore, loneliness comes from the discrepancy from what one wants and actually receives from a relationship and from neglect of basic emotional intimacy.

Angelo S. Bolea, Ph.D., is Psychologist, Private Practice, Far Horizons, Port Wing, WI 54864.

15

Effort was made to distinguish between loneliness and depression in children by closely examining the quantity and quality of interpersonal relationships. If there was a discrepancy between what children perceived and what was actually observed in terms of quality of relationship (such as a discounting of a relationship by a child or a grandiose description of their relationship) then consideration was given that those children may be experiencing loneliness even though they were not able to verbalize those feelings. If there was a disruption of a close relationship (such as through geographical change), loneliness was considered the potential outcome. If, however, there were chronic vegetative signs such as loss of appetite over a long period of time and suicidal gesture or suicidal ideation, then this type of behavior is to be classified as depression rather than loneliness. It must be granted that there may be overlapping in operationally defining differences between loneliness and depression. For the purposes of this report, distinction was made on the basis of suicidal behavior and chronic vegetative signs which were considered more depressive.

In working with children, it became clear that many children were having considerable difficulty verbalizing their thoughts and feelings about loneliness. While some of this reluctance may be due to loneliness as a generalized social stigma, behaviors of children began to cluster into categories, two of which efforts were identified as types of loneliness. Children who were experiencing difficulties with learning, not only in school but learning those things that were necessary to adjust to life, and were having very disturbed interpersonal relationships which involved either a discounting of friendship or an exaggeration of relationships were also studied. Children who have been victimized by physical and sexual abuse were also studied as experiencing a different type of loneliness.

The first type was called Learning Disability Loneliness and the second type Silent Loneliness.

LEARNING DISABILITY LONELINESS

Loneliness resulting from brain dysfunction and brain damage is a type of loneliness caused by central nervous system dysfunction, a set of internal, organic circumstances which is beyond the child's control (Osman, 1982). It essentially involves inefficiency and ineffective neuropsychological processing of information, causing not only cognitive deficits but also ineffective nonverbal reception and expression of emotional cues. These children are typically minimally verbal; surfacely defensive in attitude; and lacking in intuition, inspiration, and imagination.

These lonely children tend to violate social and emotional space and are defensive to touch (Silver, 1984). They are sometimes physically aggressive and frequently impulsive. They have difficulty giving attention, especially to auditory stimuli, and pay more attention to visual cues

(Levinson, 1984). Thus their heads may be in constant motion so that their eyes can see what their ears will only minimally hear.

While visual perception, per se, appears to be intact, spatial and auditory functioning are very weak. In this sense they are cognitively deafened. What they hear has a different meaning to them. Language and verbal mediation is distorted or weakened. The usual standardized social cues of what people say and how they say it are frequently distorted and misinterpreted. It is not uncommon for children to give a verbal recognition that is affirmative while doing just the opposite of what was presumed to have been communicated. Often the worst symptom is that these children are unaware of how different their perception of relationships can be from what actually exists.

Academically, they have difficulty starting and finishing written tasks, which is a kind of behavior that carries over into the home situation with irresponsible follow-through on household chores. Forgetfulness comes quite easily, and in fact it can be observed that these children will often forget what they are doing in the middle of carrying out various tasks. They become difficult to deal with, often generating frustration and eventual rejection from others. Soon they become frustrated with others and reciprocal rejection can occur.

More often, they are clumsy in their relationships, which turn out to be as messy as some of their written work in the academic setting. They overlook the important, necessary, small steps in making frindships and often exaggerate normal problems that occur in any developing relationship. As a result, interpersonal relationships lack depth and duration.

While these youngsters are often in a high degree of movement, especially with large, gross motor activity, fine-precision motor activity is very disrupted. They are defensive to any pencil-type tasks. They are at their worst when auditory instruction is given which needs to be completed in a written manner. This attacks the weakest connection in these learning-disabled children between the auditory input which is weak and their frustrated experience with fine graphomotor tasks. The organic connections between the auditory and fine-precision motor activity is very dysfunctional. In short, they live with cortical deafness and dysgraphia.

Pervasive throughout this type of child is gross denial. When approached about their relationships with others, they become very defensive. They are unable to give sufficient attention to verbal instructions regarding the nature of friendships, which often lack depth and duration. Their denial is considered to be organic, similar to that often expressed with right-cerebral-hemisphere dysfunction (Burns, 1985). These children are judged to have an intense sense of loneliness which is hidden behind organic denial, unverbalized but expressed in acting-out behavior. Their friendships are transient and lack emotional depth, or they are basically friendless.

SILENT LONELINESS

Silent Loneliness is frequently experienced by children victimized by sexual-physical abuse. For survival purposes, victimized children very quickly learn how to play "let's pretend" in order to deal with confusion and fear, and to please adults or older children. Frequently, this type of loneliness will show itself with a front of exaggerated people-pleasing behaviors. They are too mature for their age and often relate to adults of the opposite sex better than to adults of the same sex. Furthermore, they show caretaking tendencies to children younger than their chronological age.

Because they have had to develop strong role-playing characteristics, they are frequently confused as to true identity and develop a false sense of trust, often making poor judgments of persons with whom they develop this sense of false intimacy, pretending to be close but often feeling trapped in relationships that are abusive. At times they appear very lonely while at other times, they display a superficiality of positive affect.

In order to survive abuse, they have had to put on a people-pleasing front and thus have kept their loneliness silent and secretive. It is as if they have to develop a different ego state as a protection against feeling emotional pain and unbearable loneliness. Some have theorized this as a probable genesis of multiple personality (Watson, 1978). Certainly, this is an overachieving, lonely child.

RESEARCH METHOD

Out of a total of 122 subjects, four groups of children were identified. The first represented Learning Disability Loneliness (LDL) and the second, Silent Loneliness (SL). A third group was made of persons both abused as well as learning disabled (SL & LDL). A fourth comparison group was also judged to be lonely, but neither having brain dysfunction nor any suspicion of abuse.

For treatment reasons, children were divided into three age groups: early childhood ages 3 to 5; middle childhood ages 6 to 11; adolescents ages 12 to 17. Data were gathered only on the middle childhood group ($\bar{x}$ age 9, $\bar{x}$ I.Q. 105). They were matched on an equal basis with respect to socioeconomic status and sex, and all came from dysfunctional families where parents were either divorced or separated.

All children were seen in therapy on a weekly basis for hour-long, 20 to 40 sessions. One week they were seen individually, and the following week they were seen in group therapy. The makeup of the therapy groups were homogeneous by age; however, both girls and boys experiencing a variety of adjustment problems were included in these small groups of three to five members.

Diagnostic placement of the children into either the Learning Disability or Silent Loneliness categories was made on the basis of well-documented history of sexual abuse and an extensive battery of neuropsychological testing using the Halstead-Reitan Battery (Reitan & Davidson, 1974) and the Luria-Christensen Assessment (Christiansen, 1975). Typically these children have difficulty with auditory reversal such as that of digits backwards on typical digit-span tests (Diller, 1972). They also have difficulty reconstructing designs and performed poorly on the Tactile Perception Test, especially with the left hand. They also have difficulty with motor-shifting exercises. Children of the Learning Disability Group demonstrated lack of fluency in reading and problems with comprehension as well as difficulties with spelling and writing. Children of the Silent Loneliness Group sometimes were underachievers but showed no signs of learning disorder. Children who were both abused and learning disordered scored poorly on the neuropsychological evaluation.

TESTING INSTRUMENT

One of the major problems in studying loneliness in children is obtaining objective data through a psychological instrument. Because of the close correlation between self-concept and loneliness (Loucks, 1980) and because we are dealing with a population of youngsters who would have difficulty with verbalization, the Pictorial Self-Concept Scale (Bolea, Felker, & Barnes, 1971, currently being revised by Bolea) was selected as a measure to estimate loneliness. Furthermore, a subcomponent of Affectional Relationships was built into the original scale and seemed to be ideally suited to measuring friendships, so critical with respect to loneliness.

All children sorted out 50 picture cards of children in a variety of situations into two categories, namely "like me" and "not like me." A self-disclosure score and a self-deception score were derived from the scale according to the weighted self-concept value attached to each card.

HYPOTHESES

I. It is first hypothesized that a Learning Disability type of loneliness will yield a low self-disclosure score (total values of "like me" cards) and a high self-deception score (total value of "not like me" cards). It was reasoned that because of organic, neuropsychological involvement that denial and defensive attitude will make self-disclosure low and self-deception high.

II. It is further hypothesized that the Silent Loneliness Group will yield high self-disclosure and low self-deception but less than expected from a General Loneliness Group.

III. Those children experiencing both Learning Disability and Silent Loneliness will show results similar to the Learning Disability Group because the organic nature of the neuropsychological involvement will take antecedent precedence over abuse which is experiential.

IV. The General Loneliness Category without abuse or brain dysfunction will yield high self-disclosure and low self-deception scores.

V. Children who are judged by three different independent raters as having made progress in therapy will show a tendency toward scores like those of the Generalized Loneliness Category thus showing awareness and acceptance of loneliness, overcoming neuropsychological and psychological factors.

TECHNIQUES FOR TREATING
LEARNING DISABILITY LONELINESS

The nature of the Learning Disability Loneliness Group (LDL) was such as to warrant dealing wth the neuropsychological aspects of this loneliness first. In all, therapy was designed to enhance cerebral functioning and to circumvent organic denial (Burns, 1985).

Stage I: Recognition and Acceptance

During the initial stage of treatment, the objective was to provide experiences with immediate feedback that would encourage youngsters to recognize the difficulties they were having in establishing friendships and in maintaining friendships. To some degree, several youngsters were learning for the first time what a genuine friendship really is. After recognizing the ingredients of friendships and recognizing their trouble with friends, then it became important to provide experiences that would work at accepting their friendship deficit. Since it was believed that the neuropsychological involvement was primary in causing their denial and defensiveness, and since verbal skills were minimal, talking was kept to a minimum at first, while actions and movement were maximized (Pesso, 1969). A multisensory approach (Rubin, 1974) was definitely in order, calling for play therapy (Schafer, 1983) and art therapy which included drawings and working with clay. It was felt that nonverbal activity would appropriately stimulate compensatory processing cerebral dysfunction, predominantly of the right cerebral hemisphere (Myklebust, 1967). Spatial enhancement was encouraged by making all communication visible and concrete. Numerous pictures were produced, shared with group members, and placed on display by the child.

Activities were changed frequently in the group every 15 minutes:

working together, working alone, cooperative activities, vigorous activity play, and closing the session with relaxation training. Individual sessions were utilized to reinforce the group session by continuing art therapy activity and introducing a stepwise plan of verbalization so that success was assured along the way.

Verbalization was started gradually through first labeling (as in cartoon fashion) their works of art in terms of activity and feelings shown in the art work. Since children were very defensive, pencils, thick felt-tip pens, and extra large pieces of paper were used. Some children had already become so defensive with respect to all precision motor efforts that the therapist would often demonstrate a very flexible attitude toward drawings by crumpling the therapist's own efforts at drawing and tossing the paper away in the trash only to sit down and start over again, perhaps with a different drawing. This was an attempt to allow complete freedom of expression and frustration, with the understanding that releasing such feelings would permit eventual acceptance of their difficulty with spatial relationships. Labeling the drawings with a particular thought or feeling followed the principle of simultaneous pairing of non-verbal to verbal connections. It is believed that the right hemisphere is first stimulated (Christiansen, 1985) and thus verbal identification took place secondary to nonverbal presentation.

A second step increased verbalization by structuring a radio-announcer disc-jockey type of activity, namely mimicking a disc jockey and making announcements of pop tunes similar to what they were listening to during the group. Some children made tapes of themselves as disc jockeys. Often, current songs that described loneliness were given special attention in order to begin verbal sensitivity to feelings. It was surprising how many popular songs were readily available.

A third step of verbalization took place with the use of an intercom telephone. One child would go into a different room and call over the phone to another person in the clinic, telling them of the picture or activity he or she had completed, with prearranged structured positive feedback from the listener. Children found it much more easy to communicate over a phone to someone than they did talking with someone with visual contact. In fact, efforts were made to follow a plan of gradually leaning away from visual dependency by gradually introducing activities that would deliberately omit visual contact. The intercom worked out very well in both screening out visual cues and increasing verbalization. Other activities that reduced visual involvement included playfully attempting to copy a portion of the drawing with an opaque screening between the hand and the eyes. Other activities included play activity in the gameroom and playroom, sometimes with the lights off, in order to practice increased awareness to the kinesthetic world. Later in the treatment, auditory instructions were given to children to move in one direction or another in order to complete a maze which they walk through in a dimly lit playroom. Eventually the children became more aware and less defensive and more likely to verbalize.

Stage II: Reaching Out for Intimacy

The first step in resolving loneliness is to develop intimacy, and in order for this to happen, socialization skills were needed. Listening and leadership were taught and practiced by coaching each child, sometimes actually requiring that the child repeat what and how the coach therapist had said (Oden, 1977). It was very important to distinguish a different location (spatial differentiation) for each activity, such as the alone time, to set the groundwork for later making cognitive distinction between aloneness and loneliness (Suedfeld, 1980). Different heights of chairs and sometimes color-coded objects were used in order to distinguish between concepts such as talking and listening. It was also important to concretize such concepts as focusing on one's self as compared to focusing on another person. No more than 5 or 10 minutes were set aside for each concept, such as talking about one's self as compared to talking about what the other person had said or done. New self-cooperative play skills were taught (Currier, 1985). It was at this point in therapy that activities were directly targeted toward dealing with loneliness. Children began to express their feelings by drawing faces and images of people feeling lonely and alone versus satisfied and alone, as well as numerous other feelings. Verbalization such as "I feel something missing," "I feel as far away as another planet," and sadness with tearfulness can replace defensiveness.

Eventually, less movement and more talking was done in therapy sessions until normal approximation of interpersonal sharing and revealing of personal feelings took place verbally. This neuropsychological model (Heilman, & Satz 1983) insists that action versus usual talking therapy dominate the sessions in order to enhance the spatial, right-cerebral hemisphere so that the loneliness can be first identified nonverbally, expressed, and then healed through social communication and eventual intimacy.

TECHNIQUES FOR TREATING SILENT LONELINESS

Specific therapeutic techniques were employed to deal with the Silent Loneliness Group. First, it was felt important to take care of the safety needs of these children through developing understanding and skills with respect to taking care of their own needs. "Good and Bad Touch" program materials were utilized, teaching self-assertiveness even to the youngest child who was encouraged to memorize key phrases such as "yell and tell" (Williams, 1983). Multisensory activities were involved in a therapy process but for a different rationale (Sgroi, 1984).

It was felt that object projection was needed in order to preserve the self. As a result, dolls, stuffed animals, and sand-box play was utilized as a way of acting out, defending one's self, and expressing feelings of anger and loneliness. A role-play situation was set with three objects: the abuser, the victim, and the helper. Child and therapist made the objects (sometimes anatomically complete dolls) act out thoughts and feelings, which was the first step toward releasing fear and anger, allowing loneliness to surface.

Drawings of faces showing different feelings were done, such as that of the abuser, permitting acting out of feelings with the paper as children were encouraged to act out a complete cycle (Rubin, 1984). The former abuser was punished and rehabilitated so as to permit further self-integration of the victim who need no longer be overwhelmed by guilt and responsibility. Children were not satisifed with quick or final extermination of abusers and needed a more complete cycle before ego integration and Silent Loneliness could be released.

Special activities in preparing snacks, games for the child, and allowing the patient to prepare snacks for others was done in order to learn to distinguish between being taken care of appropriately and taking care of others in a caring manner as well as between asking and demanding. Social skills were taught to devaluate demanding, controlling, and manipulative behavior, replacing them with asking and friendly intonation. An audio tape along with a book (Currier, 1985) was utilized to continue the healing process.

The matched General Loneliness Group followed a similar multisensory approach, which was, however, much closer to traditional talking therapy such as identifying issues and expressing feelings.

SIGNIFICANT OTHERS IN TREATMENT

Parents and/or other adult caretakers of all the children met for 15 minutes before and a few minutes at the end of each individual session for feedback with respect to progress. Sharing of activities and art objects, with specific home assignments such as practicing "alone time" versus "cooperative time" and maintaining drawing and writing journals was done.

"Hands on" parenting mini-episodes took place in a role-playing manner so that adult caretakers could improve management of the children who were identified as Learning Disabled and Lonely. The caretakers were trained by the therapist in dealing with their own feelings of loneliness as well as in following through on praising youngsters for any efforts at reaching out for others, allowing and encouraging expression of loneliness, thus meeting intimacy needs and healing the loneliness.

CONCLUSION

It can be demonstrated clinically and through psychological testing that two styles of loneliness can be clearly delineated: namely Learning Disability Loneliness typified by Organic Denial treatable with activities following a Neuropsychological Model; and Silent Loneliness typified by surface people-pleasing experienced by sexually abused children treatable through Projective Play Therapy activities.

As described in the first hypothesis, Learning Disability Loneliness Group yielded a very low mean self-disclosure score when compared with either the Silent Loneliness or the General Loneliness Groups (see Table 1). It can also be demonstrated that the mean score for self-deception was much higher over the Learning Disability Group than for either the Silent Loneliness or the General Loneliness Groups. These scores would tend to support the hypothesis, that is, the type of loneliness can be identified which has denial and defensiveness as pervasive, apparently covering a hidden degree of loneliness since treatment effects did produce differences.

After treatment, the mean of disclosure score for Learning Disability Loneliness Group was much higher than before treatment and began to move in the direction approximating that of the mean self-disclosure score of children in a General Loneliness Group who had also finished treatment. Furthermore, their mean self-deception score lowered in the hypothesized direction. This means that children not only can be identified as defensively lonely but can also be taught about how to deal with loneliness through a carefully designed psychotherapy treatment process following a Neuropsychological Model.

The second hypothesis dealt with the Silent Loneliness Group which did in fact yield a relatively high mean self-disclosure and a low self-deception score but not as high or low when compared with the General Loneliness Group. However, at the completion of treatment, mean self-disclosure and self-deception scores approximated that of a General Loneliness Group which had also completed treatment.

Apparently what happens to the General Loneliness Group at the end of treatment is that they are showing less loneliness than at the onset of treatment, thus indicating a continued willingness to admit to loneliness but not at such an intense level which called for psychotherapy. Children who have been abused were unwilling to share their loneliness through their behavior and verbalization but were willing through a Pictorial Self-Concept measure to show loneliness.

Table 1

PICTORIAL SELF-CONCEPT TEST SCORES

	Self-Disclosure			Self-Deception			Progress Self-Disclosure			Progress Self-Deception		
	N	$\overline{X}$	SD	N	$\overline{X}$	SD	N	$\overline{X}$	SD	N	$\overline{X}$	SD
I. Learning Disability Loneliness	16	419	80	16	849	60	17	621	203	17	653	204
II. Silent Loneliness	13	967	99	13	307	101	13	865	335	13	409	341
III. Combined Learning Disability Loneliness and Silent Loneliness	18	336	222	18	934	203	19	810	605	19	463	307
IV. General Loneliness (Not Abused or Learning Disabled)	12	1125	98	12	149	99	14	847	159	14	436	171

25

The third hypothesis described children who were both learning disabled and abused. The hypothesis was supported insomuch that their mean self-disclosure scores and self-deception scores were very similar to the Learning Disability Loneliness Group, and this was interpreted to mean that there may well be an underlying organic factor which causes these children to present themselves with a strong sense of denial and defensiveness while either being unaware of or keeping secret inner loneliness. Nevertheless, after treatment their mean self-disclosure and self-deception scores approximated the General Loneliness Group at the end of treatment even more than either the Learning Disability or the Silent Loneliness Groups did independently.

Essentially the Learning Disability and combined Learning Disability and Silent Loneliness Groups followed a personal change similar to blocking. Others have reported this takes place with right cerebral disorders (Christiansen, 1985). A video tape presentation of an adult closed-head-injury patient by Christiansen clearly demonstrates the human interaction and development that occurs through recovery.

Scores on a Pictorial Self-Concept measure reflected levels of Self-Disclosure and Self-Deception consistent with the style of loneliness hypothesized and also reflected change toward expressing, accepting, and healing of loneliness through establishment of intimacy. Further refinement of a Pictorial Self-Concept measure that can yield a Loneliness Factor is a definite need as more research is conducted applying direct measures to understand more about the development of Childhood Loneliness and Intimacy.

REFERENCES

Asher, S.R. & Renfrew, P.D. (1981). Children without friends: Social knowledge and social skills training. In S.R. Asher & J.M. Gottman (Eds.), *The development of children's friendships.* New York: Cambridge University Press.

Bolea, A.S., Felker, D.W., & Barnes, M.D. (1971). A pictorial self-concept scale for children in K-4. *Journal of Educational Measurement.*

Burns, M.S., Harper, A.S., & Mogil, S.I. (1985). *Clinical management of right hemisphere dysfunction.* Maryland.

Christiansen, A.L. (1975). *Luria's neuropsychological investigation.* Halstead Press.

Christiansen, A.L. (1985). *Keys to clinical wisdom.* Workshop presentation, California Neuropsychology Services, San Rafael, CA.

Confer, W.M. & Ables, B.S. (1983). *Multiple personality: Etiology, diagnosis, and treatment.* New York: Human Sciences Press.

Currier, J. (1985). *Wellinworld.* Old Greenwich, CT.

Diller, L. & Weinberg, J. (1972). Differential aspects of attention in brain-damaged persons. *Perceptual and Motor Skills.*

Heilman, K.M. & Satz, P. (1983). *Neuropsychology of human emotion.* New York: Guilford Press.

Levinson, H.N. (1984). *Smart but feeling dumb.* New York: Warner Books.

Louckes, S. (1980). Loneliness, affect and self-concept: Construct validity of the Bradley Loneliness Scale. *Journal of Personality Assessment.*

Myklebust, H.R. & Johnson, D.J. (1967). *Learning disability.* New York: Grune & Stratton.

Oden, S. & Asher, S.R. (1977). Coaching children in social skills for friendship making. *Child Development*.

Osman, B.B. (1982). *No one to play with*. New York: Random House.

Peplau, L.A. & Perlman, D. (1982). *Loneliness: A source of current theory, research, and therapy*. New York: John Wiley & Sons.

Pesso, A. (1969). *Movement in psychotherapy: Psychomotor techniques and training*. New York: New York University Press.

Reitan, R.M. & Davison, L.A. (1974). *Clinical neuropsychology: Current status and applications*. New York: Winston and Sons.

Rubin, J.A. (1984). *Child art therapy: Understanding and helping children grow through art*. New York: Van Nostrand-Reinhold.

Schaefer, C.E. & O'Connor, K.J. (1983). *Handbook of play therapy.*New York: John Wiley & Sons.

Sgroi, S.M. (1984). *Handbook of clinical intervention in child sexual abuse*. Washington, DC: Heath & Co.

Silver, L.B. (1984). *The misunderstood child: A guide for parents of learning-disabled children*. New York: McGraw Hill.

Suedfeld, P. (1980). *Restricted environmental stimulation: Research and clinical applications*. New York: John Wiley & Sons.

Watkins, J.G. (1978). *The therapeutic self*. New York: Human Sciences Press.

Williams, J. (1983). *Red flag green flag people*. Rape and Abuse Crisis Center of Fargo-Moorhead, ND.

Loneliness and the Single, the Widowed, and the Divorced

Carole A. Rayburn

ABSTRACT. Little has appeared in the literature on psychotherapeutic treatment of loneliness in the single, the widowed, and the divorced. Further, not enough clarification of the differences in loneliness in these three groups has been evidenced. This article attempts to clarify such differences, reviewing some definitions and attributions of loneliness, discussing gender differences and marital status in loneliness. Clinical cases for each of the three groups are presented. Psychotherapy with the lonely is discussed, with stress on the needs and concerns of the lonely and cautions for the therapist in working with lonely patients. 53 references.

Loneliness is a phenomenon which has been seen as widely distributed and deeply distressing (Weiss, 1973) and a significant clinical problem (Fromm-Reichmann, 1959). No single cause and single solution to loneliness have emerged. Much of the recent research on loneliness has been done with college students, employing the UCLA Loneliness Scale as one of the measures. Notable is the paucity of data on psychotherapeutic intervention for lonely patients. Strategies need to be developed for dealing with those aspects of loneliness which have been supported in the literature. More specifically, little has appeared in the literature on psychotherapeutic treatment of loneliness in the single, the widowed, and the divorced. Further, not enough clarification of the differences in loneliness in these three groups has been evidenced.

SOME DEFINITIONS OF "LONELINESS"

Various definitions of "loneliness" have arisen. Loneliness has been viewed as a lack of the opportunity to relate to others on an intimate level (Jong-Gierveld, 1978; Sernat, 1978); a lack of opportunity to be able to express one's emotions and thoughts freely and without fear of misunder-

Carole A. Rayburn, Ph.D., is a clinical and consulting psychologist in private practice. She is president of the Section on the Clinical Psychology of Women, of the APA Division of Clinical Psychology (1983-1985). Requests for reprints should be addressed to: Carole A. Rayburn, Ph.D., 1200 Morningside Drive, Silver Spring, MD 20904.

standing or rejection (Sermat, 1978); the condition in which there is a disagreeable or unacceptable lag experienced between realized and desired interpersonal relationships (Jong-Gierveld, 1978); a lack of intimacy (Williams & Solano, 1983); and a state of feeling incomplete (Seligson, 1983). Further, some investigators have cautioned that assumed needs for social contact are not important, but rather individuals' desires and preferences for social relations are the vital elements in determining the presence of loneliness (Peplau & Caldwell, 1978). In this regard, loneliness has been differentiated from aloneness, solitude, and social isolation, all of which may be considered desireable at times by individuals (Lowenthal, 1964; Weiss, 1973; and Peplau & Caldwell, 1978). Others have seen it as social isolation (Jong-Gierveld, 1978).

SOME ATTRIBUTES OF THE LONELY

Jong-Gierveld (1978) considers loneliness to be multidimensional. To her, loneliness involves feelings of deprivation (further subdivided into types and intensity of deprivation and reactions to the deprivation; and adjustment and defense mechanisms) and ways in which feelings of deprivation are seen in a future perspective (divided into infinite or finite time perspective; and the individual's ability or inability, alone or with others, to bring about a change in the situation of loneliness, that is, to control the situation. Moore and Schultz (1983), in a study of loneliness at adolescence, found that loneliness was positively related to state and trait anxiety, social anxiety, self-consciousness, depression, and an external locus of control. It was negatively related, however, to self-reported likability, attractiveness, happiness, and life satisfaction. Lonely adolescents were less likely to take risks than nonlonely adolescents. Schultz and Moore (1984) found that less willingness to take risks was also found in lonely older adults who were 55-75 years old; in this older population, loneliness was attributed to being without others and thought to be aggravated by social isolation and inaction. As among college and adolescent populations, then, loneliness in older persons was associated with higher depression and anxiety and lower levels of happiness and life satisfaction.

Schill, Toves, and Ramanaiah (1980) have suggested than an external locus of control in individuals is more helpful in coping effectively with loneliness than an internal one. They found that there were positive and significant relationships between loneliness and the number of emotional and psychosomatic complaints on the Cornell Medical Index. Another study by these researchers (1981) supported the 1980 findings.

The lonely, compared to the nonlonely, were seen as more shy (Maroldo, 1981); possessing significantly lower self-esteem (Jones, Freemon, & Goswick, 1981); being more aggressive, hostile, and resentful (Mijuskovic, 1983); less willing to self-disclose (Chelune, Sultan, &

Williams, 1980; Mahon, 1982; Solano, Batten, & Parish, 1982); having more interpersonal dependency (Mahon, 1982); showing significantly greater sensitivity to rejection by others (Jones, Freemon, & Goswick, 1981); having poorer social skills or reporting greater deficits in their social skills and other abilities (Anderson, Horowitz, & French, 1983; Jones, Freemon, & Goswick, 1981; Jones, Hobbs, & Hockenbury, 1982); evidencing negative feelings about human relationships in general and rejecting others more frequently than others rejected them (Jones, Sansone, & Helm, 1983; Jong-Gierveld, 1978; Russell, Peplau, & Cutrona, 1980); feeling more "empty" and restless (Russell, Peplau, & Cutrona, 1980); and as being separated more from meaningful interaction with others (Hecht & Baum, 1984; Wheeler, Reis, & Nezlek, 1983).

Hecht and Baum (1984), with a small but well-controlled population of young adults, found a strong and moderate relationship between early disrupted attachment and loneliness. Subjective loneliness was significantly related to emotional and social isolation and attachment-threat and quality but not to the actual number of separations. Jones (1981) studied undergraduates living at home with one or both parents and reported that their experience of loneliness had less to do with the external characteristics of the lonely person's social milieu than with the process by which the loneliness influenced how the lonely perceived, evaluated, and responded to interpersonal reality.

Corty and Young (1981) found that loneliness but not the absolute level of social contact is correlated with the perceived number of problems. Low levels of social contact were not associated with loneliness. Schultz and Saklofske (1983) found that individuals scoring low on helpfulness to others reported more loneliness than more helpful persons did. In studies of stress and religious leaders (Rayburn, 1984a, 1984b; Rayburn, Richmond, & Rogers, 1983), social support and an opportunity to take part in a religious community or in a socially supportive network or counseling group were related to less stress and more satisfying social relations as well as greater opportunities to express one's thoughts and feelings without fear of misunderstanding, rejection, or blame. In these studies, social support was especially important to women in combating felt loneliness.

GENDER DIFFERENCES IN LONELINESS

Before discussing the single, widowed, and divorced, it is helpful to understand something about gender differences in loneliness that have been reported in more recent literature. Booth (1983a) found that males were significantly more lonely than females in a study of college students, but in females the loneliness was negatively correlated with college GPA, composite American College Test scores, and IQs. However, for males the correlations were positive for ACT and for IQ when paired with loneliness scores, and negative for loneliness in males and GPA. Further, no significant differences were found for loneliness and GPA.

Schill, Toves, and Ramanaiah (1980), investigating coping with loneliness and locus of control, found that it was especially the male external subjects who seemed to be least affected by loneliness. Hansson and Jones (1981) found that, while lonely individuals had less confidence in their opinions and were less willing to verbalize their ideas in public (the first step in the social comparison process) than nonlonely persons, lonely males more than lonely females were less conforming to a social consensus when they made important judgments regarding others' welfare. The lonely males were less influenced by a model of helpful behavior in an altruism experiment. On the other hand, females who were lonely were more conforming and more apt to duplicate the responses of the model.

Jones, Sansone, and Helm (1983) had college students rate themselves and their partners on loneliness after brief interactions with opposite sex strangers. This study supported previous findings about loneliness and interpersonal judgments in relating high loneliness scores with more negative self-ratings and ratings expected from partners. Further, it extended other findings in that men only showed higher loneliness ratings related to more negative ratings of partners. Lonely men were rated more negatively by partners than were nonlonely men, but this effect was not found for women. In general, lonely men and women were viewed by their partners as more apt to rate themselves negatively.

In a study of loneliness, sex roles, and social interaction, Wheeler, Reis, and Nezlek (1983) found that both men and women showed a negative relationship between loneliness and the amount of time spent with females and between loneliness and the meaningfulness of interaction with both sexes. Notably, meaningfulness with males was more important than meaningfulness with females, with femininity being associated negatively to loneliness for men and women. Gender differences were seen in the degree to which variables overlapped in predictions of loneliness: one group of nonlonely men had meaningful relationships with men and with women, whereas another group of nonlonely men related meaningfully only with men. For women, one nonlonely group had meaningful relationships with men only, but another group of nonlonely women related meaningfully to women only. There was little variance for women who related meaningfully to both men and women.

Jones, Freemon, and Goswick (1981) also found that lonely persons rated themselves and others more negatively and expected others to rate them negatively (which was not supported by actual ratings except for the initial part of group interactions and by other lonely people after dyadic interactions). In men, loneliness was negatively associated with expressed inclusion and to expressed affection and to desired affection. Lonely men were less assertive, preferred to be alone more often and to maintain affectional distance from others. Lonely women showed their loneliness to be correlated with wanted control, control interchange, and private self-consciousness. Loneliness was thus seen as social inadequacy, but there was little to indicate that lonelier people were less interested in social involvement. Moreover, loneliness was related negatively to self-perceptions and one's social skills. Lonely men especially tend to rate lonely women as less socially responsive. Gender differences in openness and in effects of loneliness on observers' skills in detecting loneliness were suggested as explanations for gender differences in loneliness.

Concerning loneliness, self-disclosure, and gender differences, Chelune, Sultan, and Williams (1980) suggested that lonely women may experience special problems in establishing new relationships in novel situations: One group may have difficulty regulating self-disclosure and may withdraw from social activities, while the other group may be more socially skilled and participate in increased levels of social interactions. Solano, Batten, and Parish (1982) found that loneliness was linearly and significantly related to self-perceived lack of intimate disclosure to opposite-sex friends for men and women. Perceived lack of self-disclosure to same-sex friends was also associated with loneliness for women. For men, loneliness was most likely to be related to low self-disclosure in cross-sex relationships. Self-disclosing to both female and male friends was related to intimacy needs in women. As in Chelune et al., lonely women and men had lower levels of intimate disclosure to opposite-sex friends. Women who are lonely are more unwilling to disclose to men. A low level of self-disclosure was associated with loneliness by women but not by men. It was suggested that women but not men may expect to participate in intimate conversations with same-sex friends more often in their lives.

In studies of gender differences and loneliness, perhaps the more interesting and challenging are those concerning androgyny. Avery (1982) studied loneliness in adolescence and found that androgynous people were significantly less lonely than masculine, feminine, and undifferentiated persons. Males more than females were affected by the impact of sex-role orientation on loneliness. Thus, androgyny (high masculinity—high feminity) is more closely related to social adjustment and less loneliness than masculinity (high masculinity—low femininity), femininity (high femininity—low masculinity), and undifferentiated (low masculinity—low femininity) sex-role orientations.

Berg and Peplau (1982) found that for young adults, loneliness was negatively correlated with past disclosure, willingness to disclose, and social responsiveness for women only. While high masculinity or high femininity were initially thought to ward off loneliness, androgynous in-

dividuals were least lonely. Masculinity favors more risk-taking in form-
ing new social relations, thus discouraging loneliness. Emotional responsiveness and concern for others stressed by femininity encourages the
maintenance of satisfying social relations; this lowers loneliness. In both
sexes, lowered levels of loneliness were associated with high expressivity
and high instrumentality, both found in the androgynous person.

LONELINESS AND MARITAL STATUS

Wood (1978a) reported that loneliness was greater in women than in
men and greater in unmarried than in married persons in her study. Marriage may mean a loss of esteem and respect for women, in that careers
may be disrupted and social ties through one's job may end. Research
such as Weiss' (1973 pp. 10-12) has also supported the expectation of
greater benefits of marriage for men than for women as regards loneliness. Wood also found in her study that loneliness was significantly in-
versely related to self-esteem, esteem, respect, and social identity. There
was a significant interaction between sex and marital status, as well as
between sex and education, and for sex, education, and marital status.
Women who are married, and women who are married and have some
university education, are more lonely than single men and women and
married men. In younger groups of women, since women do tend to
marry at an earlier age than do men, women are not lonelier than men.
However, widowed men might be expected to have a high level of loneliness because there are fewer widowers to sympathize and strategize with
them. The differences in women and men as concerns their marital status
and education and loneliness were accounted for by expectations of
greater access to valued occupations for men than for women, with
decrease in loneliness being greatest for single educated men, less for
single educated women, even less for married men, and very least for
married women. For the educated married woman, education may not be
relevant to homemaking or employment subordinate to the homemaker
role. Further, where higher education may lead married women to expect
greater occupational and social fulfillment for themselves than is actually
the case, loneliness may increase. These conclusions assume traditional
sex-role socialization, with its tendency to broaden personal alternatives
for men but to restrict them for women.

Jong-Gierveld (1978) found marital status differences to be related to
differences in average intensity of feelings of loneliness, with higher
loneliness scores being found for unmarried, widowed, and divorced than
married people.

Austin (1983) found no significant differences by sex on the Intimate
factor of the UCLA Loneliness Scale, with men and women reporting
similarly on feelings of distance from intimate others or an absence from

significant others; the Intimate Others factor included ideas of isolation, lack of others to disclose to, and feelings of exclusion ("There is no one I can turn to"; "Nobody really knows me"; "I feel left out.") However, men significantly more than women reported more often not having Social Others (a factor involving a sense of having or not having a social network to connect with, others to talk with and to turn to) and lacking Belonging and Affiliation (feeling part of a group of friends, having a lot in common with those around oneself, being in tune with those around, not feeling alone). No significant differences were found for these factors and marital status or even with the factors and the current living arrangements of the respondents.

The Single

Wood (1978a), as mentioned, found that single women were apt to be more lonely than single men, but single women were less lonely than married women while single men were more lonely than married men. Jong-Gierveld (1978) mentioned that unmarried older persons scored higher on loneliness than married older people. Solano (1980) studied the loneliness scores of undergraduates, finding that males were more lonely on the Belcher Extended Loneliness Scale and scored higher on general loneliness and alienation than females. Further, males were lonelier in terms of pathological loneliness, existential loneliness, and loneliness depression. She suggested that the global, intuitive definition of loneliness held by college undergraduates is mainly associated with lack of social companionship.

Some Clinical Cases of the Lonely Single Person

In my private practice, I saw Joan, age 35. From the Southwest, Joan had an older brother and a younger sister. Never a popular person, she had only dated once, in her first year of college. While she claimed that she liked the young man fairly well, she did not seem to make interesting-enough conversation that he wanted to ask her out again. Socially shy anyway, she took this initial failure in the dating game as a sure sign that no one could possibly like her. She withdrew even more, applying herself more intensely to her studies. Graduating with a degree in economics, she secured a good job with the government. During her second year on the job, she met a younger woman from her home state who also was working in the office. Amy, age 26, was a lesbian who had had several lovers. When Amy befriended Joan, responding in part to the obvious loneliness unashamedly admitted by Joan, Joan was initially grateful and then quite flattered. She grew to depend on Amy to satisfy all of her emotional and sexual needs. They decided to make a commitment to each other and to live together. After 3 years of relative happiness, Amy saw Joan's dependency as rather suffocating and she decided to have another relationship on the side. This was intolerable to Joan, who had by now become extremely possessive of Amy. When tearful Joan demanded that Amy be faithful to her alone, Amy moved out of the home while continuing to work in the same office as Joan. Immediately after the breakup, Joan became seriously depressed, considered suicide, and came in for psychotherapy. Whenever she sees Amy exhibiting any friendliness to female co-workers, which Joan goes out of her way to observe, she becomes livid to the point of being irrational. Amy's superior on the job, she has threatened to "tell all" about Amy's lesbianism to their employer. Her attitude has been that (a) she cannot meet anyone else (she is hardly trying to do so, actually); (b) she could not possibly love anyone else but Amy; and (c) if she cannot have Amy, no one else can either. Thus, she allows herself to scapegoat Amy by making her the cause of her own loneliness; this allows her to escape responsibility for taking care of solving her own problems with loneliness. She resists going out to social affairs or even establishing friendly relationships with co-workers. Joan lacks social skills so needed in interpersonal relationships, she has serious unresolved anger and resentment and strong dependency needs, and a lack of self-esteem and self-confidence.

Bill, 45, grew up on his grandparents' farm and was close to his parents and two sisters and two brothers. Mutually dependent on his family, he helped them out financially until he was 30. Dating infrequently until he was 31, he left the farm when his mother died, and he came East and opened a small business. A success at business, he nonetheless did not find satisfaction in his social life. Most of the women whom he dated were not seriously interested in him. He, however, was serious about seeking and finding a marriage partner. When he apparently failed to hold the interest of his dates, he decided to take courses at the local junior colleges and adult education centers. However, he could not hide his basic shyness too well. He lacked self-esteem and self-confidence, putting himself down because he was not better educated. Bill was a chronically lonely individual, continuing to date but never seeming to find a compatible companion to share his life. In the whirl of self-improvement courses, he seldom pauses long enough to set more realistic goals for securing a lover or a mate. In such ways, he is able to perpetuate denigrating himself for his failures in the social world. He plays a perennial game of "what if . . ." and "if it weren't for . . .," not to mention "Wooden Leg."

The Widowed

Jong-Gierveld spoke of widows feeling a sense of deprivation, having feelings of missing their partners and of being abandoned. Haas-Hawkings (1978), speaking of intimacy as a moderating influence on stress of loneliness in widowhood, noted that the stronger tendency of women to maintain confidant relationships outside marriage while men rely more on their spouse for a link to outside social networks are important factors in understanding gender differences in widowhood. Loneliness has been one of the most frequently reported problems of widowhood. Some studies (Lowenthal & Haven, 1968) had involved evolving social roles, psychological adjustment to widowhood, the quality of duration of interpersonal relationships, and loneliness. In the Lowenthal and Haven investigation, while having a confidant acted as a buffer against social-role losses and the losses of the disruptive and depriving event of widowhood, individuals *without* a confidant might increase their social activities and yet be much more depressed and lonely than those *with* a confidant who decrease their interpersonal relations.

Age peers are highly important as confidants, especially for older widows, since family associations are not voluntary and may be seen as increasing dependency over relatives (Arling, 1976). In widows of age 51 and over, there may even be a time dimension in the experience of loneliness concerning widowhood: A past type of loneliness would concern thinking about the individual, life-style, or mood of one's past experience; the present loneliness would involve the current loss, deprivation, a sense of alienation, or a wish to return to happier times with the lost loved one; a future-based loneliness or "loneliness anxiety" is associated with fear of losing one's spouse coupled with the fear of not being able to begin anew and to establish other meaningful relationships (Lopata, 1969). In this same study, Lopata noted that widows may experience loneliness connected with the deceased spouse as a person, an object of affection and love, a companion, an individual who had made her the object of his love, one who had been around to organize time and work, one who shared in the division of labor, and a source of life-style and of status.

Widowers more often than widows suffer from loneliness and depression, with men being more likely than women to perceive their wives as their most and often only confidant (Lowenthal & Haven, 1968). Townsend (1957) differentiated between desolation (recent experience of becoming socially isolated, as in loss of one's spouse) and isolation (absence of social interaction); death rates were higher among older widowed individuals, particularly men.

Some Clinical Cases of Lonely Widowed Persons

Katherine was widowed fairly young in life, when she was only 30. Well educated and enjoying her profession of social work, she had a marriage considered by most as almost perfect. The oldest of two children born to parents who provided for most of her childhood needs, she had dated widely in late adolescence and early adulthood. A warm and affable yet determined and serious person, she had put her education and career first in her life and did not marry until she was 24. Family planning was delayed until both she and her husband finished their university studies. Together, Katherine and Bob enjoyed a good social life, replete with professional colleagues and others with whom they liked sharing their lives, frustrations, and aspirations. Too, both of them shared a strong religious faith. Tragedy struck suddenly: Bob fell over his desk at work with a fatal though first coronary. Katherine felt devastated. Though her faith and social network of colleagues served as somewhat of a buffer in her many hours of loneliness and desolation, she spoke bitterly of the social circle of friends whom she knew with her husband. Other couples now did not invite her to join them for social events, perhaps viewing her as an "extra" woman at affairs that were otherwise couples situations. At times, she suffers from such loneliness for Bob that she just wants to be by herself, not thinking that anyone else will really understand her pain. At other times, she throws herself into her career, her church work, and her hobbies—anything to get her mind off of her loss for even a moment. Dating is not something she even cares to think about yet, since the sting of her loss is still too fresh and her memories of Bob ever-present. She has been persuaded by a colleague to come in for psychotherapy to work through her feelings of loneliness and sadness and to gain new directions in her life's pathways.

Jean was 55 when she lost her husband. Part of a large Catholic family, she had a built-in support system. There were some problems, however, which she was not able to share with her relatives and her five children. John, her husband of 35 years, had had several sexual relationships with adolescent males. For many years, Jean closed her eyes to John's severe alcoholism. However, when he was fairly obvious about his young men, staying out late drinking with them and being openly affectionate with them in the presence of others, she was forced into the reality of his betrayal of her. Yet, a staunch and "'good Catholic,'" she continued her denial in front of her children and made excuses to them for their father's frequent absences from the home. After health problems led her to quit her job, from which she had derived much satisfaction, she was cut off from a vital network of friendly co-workers. She felt that she was very alone, not being able to turn to relatives for comfort and understanding. She felt demoralized and ashamed to even be experiencing problems. Everyone had come to depend on her as the proverbial "rock of Gibraltar" through most of her life; now that rock was showing some weathering and cracking. The "rock" began to crumble a bit when John was killed in a car accident while he drove in the snow in a drunken stupor. Haunted by tremendous guilt that she had not been able to help him more, with the possibility that John had been suicidal toward the end of his life, and that she could never work out her feelings of anger, resentment, desertion, then acceptance and love with a live husband, she came into psychotherapy. Her main concern was to overcome the loneliness and sense of bewilderment which seemed almost overwhelming for her at times. She also needed to rid herself of the guilt, anger, and sense of shame for her husband's affairs (with which she was just now getting in touch). Too, she wanted to come off the pedestal of sainthood and omnipotence upon which she had allowed herself to be placed by others. She needed, wanted, and now sought ways to constructively depend upon and receive nurturing from others.

The Divorced

Jong-Gierveld (1978) found that women who were divorced and deserted seem to be more lonely than unmarried, married, and older women. The divorced experienced missing their partner less than did widows, and divorced women tended to rationalize their feelings of loneliness more than the single or widowed. Unlike other groups of women, divorcees have less tendency to discuss feelings of being abandoned than men do. Divorced men are more likely to stress feelings of emptiness and lack of companionship.

Woodward, Zabel, and Decosta (1980) found that loneliness was associated with divorce, with women being more affected than men. The deepest feelings of loneliness concerned social situations in which women thought finances caused restrictions, and when certain tasks had to be done and they had nobody with whom to share the responsibility. Men and women experienced loneliness when they thought that they were out of place at a certain place or time.

De Grace, Joshi, and Roberge (1983) found that for divorced or separated women, loneliness decreased with the increase of time spent in marriage, as the duration of separation or divorce increased, and as time spent living apart from their husbands or ex-husbands increased. Loneliness was also lower with increased age, as in the studies of Nahemow (1979) and Rubenstein (1979).

Moulton (1980) described divorce in the middle years (35-45). Attempts at avoiding disappointments and depression during these years may result in changes in marital status. With divorce, women are often lonely and men often reluctant. She noted that seemingly strong and independent women may go through much turmoil after a divorce which they initiated, mourn their marriages, desire to return to their husbands at times, and being frustrated in attempts to remarry. Professional women longing for more satisfying lives and having a need for freedom from domesticity and greater autonomy may seek a divorce. The men whom they meet may also be divorced, quite fearful of remarriage or other long-term commitment, and fearful of a woman's dependency on them.

Divorced women may find that they still want male affection and admiration, without which they may feel lonely, isolated, and unsatisfied overall. For both sexes, she sees the quest for greater autonomy than they can handle as related to early and unsatisfactory parental relationships. Social prejudice reinforces the social isolation begun in childhood, unattached women being perceived often as a burden or threat while uncommitted men are considered an asset and a challenge.

Some Clinical Cases of Divorced Persons

George, twice divorced, is fighting for the custody of his child. Entering treatment because of his depression and anxiety about his child being placed with his mother during the divorce proceedings, he manifested deep underlying loneliness as well. He is the youngest of three sons. His mother had left the home in a stormy divorce when he was a young boy. Apparently he learned much of his obsessive-compulsive rigidity and underlying dependency on women from his father. Lonely most of his life, he did not date until his first year in college, and then very limitedly. Critical of and angry with women, as he is of his mother, he nonetheless seeks them out to lessen his great loneliness. He does this most often by being the good little boy and endearing himself for a while to the women, doing all kinds of home repairs for them. Then his fear and resentment take over, and he becomes overcritical and rigid and this angers the woman and leads her to reject him. Thus does he start the whole cycle over, experiencing loneliness, seeking female companionship, getting scared and rejected, and feeling lonely again.

Nancy married at 18 to a person whom her father strongly rejected. That seemed to be one of the primary reasons for the marriage—a rebellion against her father. She deeply resented her father's coldness toward her and her mother, yet she came from a traditional home where she had been scripted to depend on men and to seek marriage. After 3 years of a rather meaningless relationship with an inconsiderate and immature husband, she got a divorce. Almost immediately, a profound loneliness came over her and she withdrew in confusion as to what to do. While she attended college classes and kept trim at the spa, she was not able to find the thing she wanted most: a caring man who would share his life with her. Now, at age 30, she maintains her relationships with several women friends but seems to attract only immature, selfish, and noncommitted men. Never really satisfied, she has dates but no meaningful interactions with men. There is still too much discrepancy between what she says she needs and what she neurotically seeks and finds.

Don, 45, is the second son of a fundamentalist minister. Married for 21 years and the father of two children, he was faced with uninvited divorce after his wife decided to run off with her lover. Although a theology professor, he found that his divorce resulted in his being placed on indefinite leave of absence from his job and that the greatest source of comfort to him—his church and other church members—were totally unsupportive of him because of their felt threat of divorce. Thus, he has suddenly lost many social support systems on which he had come to depend. The result has been much loneliness and depression, which he has partially sought to resolve by throwing himself into a new job. Too, there is the loneliness of being separated from his children. He is just now dealing more effectively with his anger, hurt pride, and feelings of abandonment; and he is considering dating again.

PSYCHOTHERAPY WITH THE LONELY

As has been noted by several researchers, lonely people often have low self-esteem and low self-confidence. It is important that therapists avoid blaming the lonely for their predicament (Wood, 1978b). Lonely people themselves may ask three quesitons: Who is to blame? Will it change? What control do I have? Whereas the self-blame of alienated (those never developing and maybe not desiring close relationships) and defeated (those, usually married and then divorced, who tried but failed to have lasting relationships) lonely people may be related to greater withdrawal than blaming others, blaming others may be associated with lonely persons who are hostile and resentful (Peplau & Caldwell, 1978).

Sermat (1978) pointed out the irony of our contemporary culture which engenders the belief that individuals do not owe anything to anyone else, while at the same time they seek satisfaction, security and meaning through relationships with others. Fear of commitment to others, fearing that they will want too much and restrict one's freedom, may well be a factor in loneliness and the single and the divorced. Jerome (1983) also stressed the need of the lonely to develop more realistic attitudes about personal relationships, learning not only exclusive and egoistic but also reciprocal and altruistic modes of interaction. In that study, lonely women who joined a social club found that the club required social skills that its members did not have. Others (Booth, 1983b; Peplau, Russell, & Heim, 1979) have commented on loneliness resulting from interpersonal expectations not fitting interpersonal reality.

Booth (1983b) and Roth (1983) noted the problem therapists may have in resisting recognition of loneliness in patients in an effort to deny or defend against their own loneliness; in this way, therapists may miss important cues that indicate the patient is indeed lonely, whether or not this is verbalized directly. Yet, there is another facet of working with the lonely which therapists must both be aware of and guard against: needing to help the patient to overcome the loneliness and its detrimental effects without

being seduced as therapists into the role of supreme rescuer for the seemingly helpless, sometimes childlike and "victimized" lonely individual.
Certainly, lonely patients do not really benefit from such "protection,"
most especially if this gets into sexual behavior between therapist and patient. Thus, it would be not only prudent but most ethical for therapists to
adhere completely to the kinds of guidelines proposed by the American
Psychological Association Division of Counseling Psychology (1978) for
doing therapy with women (but the principles could be broadened for men
in therapy as well). Neither avoiding the fact of loneliness nor avoiding
the lonely patient will result in effective therapy, but neither will it help to
still the tears or painful sighs of such persons by any sexually suggestive
parenting.

Beyond the necessity for nonsexist therapy for the lonely, the therapist
would do well to teach the patient something about assertiveness and
other social skills, two real protections against deep loneliness. Lonely
men as well as lonely women need to learn to assert themselves more in
interpersonal interactions. They need to learn more effective strategies of
talking to others: role-playing conversations between them and same-sex
and opposite-sex others will enable them to practice their social skills and
to feel more comfortable in initiating an interchange and self-disclosing.
As noted, lonely individuals do not tend to take many risks. They need to
be encouraged to gradually take more risks, including those involved in
self-disclosure. Desensitization techniques could be useful here in working on lowering potential threats in taking risks. Learning to self-disclose
more will come after the lonely person has decided to take more risks in
trusting others, beginning with the therapist and any significant others.
Self-disclosing would provide an opportunity for the lonely to relate to
and identify with the human family and its conditions.

While lonely people tend to be dependent on others, the therapist
should discourage overdependence of the patient on the therapist and on
others. Therapy techniques using rational-emotive therapy, for instance,
could be beneficial in working on the irrational thinking in these individuals. Getting them to ask themselves why they look for *blame* for their
loneliness in themselves and why they may blame others (instead of con-
structively seeking options to nonproductive behavior in relating to others
and in living with oneself); helping them to catastrophize less about their
problems and to realize that they can take more control of their difficult
life circumstances and change the outcomes more often; helping them to
better reflect upon their feelings of low self-esteem and low self-confidence as these may be related to irrational thinking; and being more realistic in terms of their expressions of anger and resentment and of their expectations of life and of other people would be necessary conditions for
doing good therapy with the lonely.

The lonely often have quite unrealistic expectations, looking for the
perfect mate, the ideal spouse or infallible lover, the completely satis-

fying job, the totally fulfilling friendship, that is, the irrationality that everything that one might *like* to be actually *must* be. In the same way, the lonely individual sets unrealistic goals and self-images: one must be attractive, fairly wealthy, highly intelligent, witty, and charming before one can really succeed in relationships with others. If one is married, one must be Super-Woman or Super-Man. A parent must be Super-Mom or -Dad. Such locked-in rigidity is also related to and hindering of risk-taking.

Not only do lonely people need to stop blaming themselves, but they need to resist accepting blame from others. As a group, they are more sensitive than nonlonely persons to rejection from others. Helping them to confront the irrational thinking on such ready acceptance of blame and rejection would enhance the building of self-esteem and self-confidence within them. Assigning them "homework" tasks of verbalizing at least one idea of their own in public a week would help them to build on their competency and confidence.

They need to learn not to think catastrophically about being alone, about thinking that they need to be with another person all of the time, or about not having others on whom to depend heavily. Along with learning to be more independent and liking it, lonely persons need to be more motivated by altruism: they need to be more helpful to others and not to just depend on receiving help from others.

Discussing strategies for developing a social network is effective in therapy with the lonely. Men often depend on their wives or lovers as primary confidants. They may have a network at their jobs, but this usually vanishes upon retirement. Then men may have fewer resources, especially if they are single (never having married) or widowed. For women, widowhood or divorce may necessitate getting employment as soon as possible. The therapist could help these women to develop strategies for reentry into the workforce, or may refer the patient to a vocational guidance counselor for this. Women may need to acquire more job-training skills and education, and the realistic expectations about these areas of concern need to be discussed in therapy with lonely women, whether single, married, widowed, or divorced. Married persons, especially women, should be encouraged to establish new and maintain old social networks. For educated women, gatherings of college women in American Association of University Women types of meetings, where they can exchange intellectual pursuits and hone their mental prowess would not only provide a social network but help to meet the needs of these women to express themselves professionally and intellectually. These kinds of meetings should be especially encouraged for married women with some college training who may have little interpersonal interaction with others if they do not work outside the home, if they have children at home, or even if they have routine or unrewarding jobs.

If women do wish to work at outside employment, they need to learn what the most realistic job is for their level of training and education, as well as preferences, and to feel all right for not restricting themselves to work in the home. Training them in assertiveness is very important here. Therapists who provide their patients with themselves as role-models of assertive behavior would enable the lonely to become less lonely and more potent. These strategies engender behavior within individuals that allow them to take better care of themselves. Single persons often find more time to set aside to improve themselves and to see this as necessary for their emotional well-being and self-respect. Encouraging androgynous interests of men and women would also enhance their spectrum of activities and increase their coping mechanisms in overcoming loneliness.

REFERENCES

American Psychological Association, Division on Counseling Psychology. (1978, Dec.). Principles concerning the counseling and therapy of women. *APA Monitor*.

Anderson, C. A., Horowitz, L. M., & French, R. D. (1983). Attributional style of lonely and depressed people. *Journal of Personality and Social Psychology, 45*(1), 127-136.

Arling, G. (1976). The elderly widow and her family, neighbors and friends. *Journal of Marriage and the Family, 38*, 757-768.

Austin, B. A. (1983). Factorial structure of the UCLA Loneliness Scale. *Psychological Reports, 53*, 883-889.

Avery, A. W. (1982). Escaping loneliness in adolescence: The case for androgyny. *Journal of Youth and Adolescence, 11*(6), 451-459.

Berg, J. H. & Peplau, L. A. (1982). Loneliness: The relationship of self-disclosure and androgyny. *Personality and Social Psychology Bulletin, 8*(4), 624-630.

Booth, R. (1983a). An examination of college GPA, composite ACT scores, IQs, and gender in relation to loneliness of college students. *Psychological Reports, 53*(2), 347-352.

Booth, R. (1983b). Toward an understanding of loneliness. *Social Work, 28*(1), 116-119.

Chelune, G. J., Sultan, F. E., & Williams, C. L. (1980). Loneliness, self-disclosure, and interpersonal effectiveness. *Journal of Consulting Psychology, 27*(5), 462-468.

Corty, E. & Young, R. D. (1981). Social contact and perceived loneliness in college students. *Perceptual and Motor Skills, 53*(3), 773-774.

De Grâce, G. R., Joshi, P., & Roberge, L. (1983). Loneliness and nonverbal communication in separated or divorced women: An exploratory study. *Psychological Reports, 53*, 151-154.

Fromm-Reichmann, F. (1959). On loneliness. In D.M. Bullard (Ed.), *Psychoanalysis and psychotherapy, Selected papers of Frieda Fromm-Reichmann* (pp. 325-336). Chicago: University of Chicago Press.

Haas-Hawkings, G. (1978). Intimacy as a moderating influence on the stress of loneliness in widowhood. *Essence, 2*(4), 249-258.

Hansson, R. O. & Jones, W. H. (1981). Loneliness, cooperation, and conformity among American undergraduates. *Journal of Social Psychology, 115*(1), 103-108.

Hecht, D. T. & Baum, S. K. (1984). Loneliness and attachment patterns in young adults. *Journal of Clinical Psychology, 40*(1), 193-197.

Jerome, D. (1983). Lonely women in a friendship club. *British Journal of Guidance and Counselling, 11*(1), 10-20.

Jones, W. H. (1981). Loneliness and social contact. *Journal of Social Psychology, 113*(2), 295-296.

Jones, W. H., Freemon, J. E., & Goswick, R. A. (1981). The persistence of loneliness: Self and other determinants. *Journal of Personality, 49*(1), 27-48.

Jones, W. H., Hobbs, S. A., & Hockenbury, D. (1982). Loneliness and social skill deficits. *Journal of Personality and Social Psychology, 42*(4), 682-689.

Jones, W. H., Sansone, C., & Helm, B. (1983). Loneliness and interpersonal judgments. *Personality and Social Psychology Bulletin, 9*(3), 437-441.

Jong-Gierveld, J. (1978). The construct of loneliness: Components and measurement. *Essence, 2*(4), 221-237.

Lopata, H. Z. (1969). Loneliness: Forms and components. *Social Problems, 17*, 248-261.

Lowenthal, M. F. (1964). Social isolation and mental illness in old age. *American Sociological Review, 29*, 54-70.

Lowenthal, M. F. & Haven, C. (1968). Interaction and adaption: Intimacy as a critical variable. *American Sociological Review, 33*, 20-30.

Mahon, N. E. (1982). The relationship of self-disclosure, interpersonal dependency, and life changes to loneliness in young adults. *Nursing Research, 31*(6), 343-347.

Maroldo, G. (1981). Shyness and loneliness among college men and women. *Psychological Reports, 48*(3), 885-886.

Mijuskovic, B. (1983). Loneliness and hostility. *Psychology: A Quarterly Journal of Human Behavior, 20*(3-4), 9-19.

Moore, D. & Schultz, N. R. (1983). Loneliness at adolescence: Correlates, attributions, and coping. *Journal of Youth and Adolescence, 12*(2), 95-100.

Moulton, R. (1980). Divorce in the middle years: The lonely woman and the reluctant man. *Journal of the American Academy of Psychoanalysis, 8*(2), 235-250.

Nahemow, N. (1979). Residence, kinship and social isolation among the aged Baganda. *Journal of Marriage and the Family, 41*, 171-183.

Peplau, L. A. & Caldwell, M. A. (1978). Loneliness: A cognitive analysis. *Essence, 2*(4), 207-220.

Peplau, L. A., Russell, D., & Heim, M. (1979). An attributional analysis of loneliness. In I. H. Frieze, D. Bar-Tal, & J. S. Carroll (Eds.), *Attribution theory: Application to social problems* (pp. 53-78). New York: Jossey-Bass.

Rayburn, C. A. (1984a). Clergywomen, clergymen, and their spouses: Stress in the religious. Paper presented at the International Council of Psychologists Annual Convention, Mexico City, Mexico.

Rayburn, C. A. (1984b). Stress in clergy couples: Clergy married to clergy. Paper presented at the International Council of Psychologists Annual Convention, Mexico City, Mexico.

Rayburn, C. A., Richmond, L. J., & Rogers, L. (1983). Stress among religious leaders. *Thought, 58* (230), 329-344.

Roth, N. (1983). Loneliness and the poet: Robert W. Services. *Journal of the American Academy of Psychoanalysis, 11*(4), 593-602.

Rubenstein, C. M. (1979). A questionnaire study of adult loneliness in three U.S. cities. *Dissertation Abstracts* International, 40 (5-B), 2439.

Russell, D., Peplau, L. A., & Cutrona, C. (1980). The Revised UCLA Loneliness Scale: Concurrent and discriminant validity evidence. *Journal of Personality and Social Psychology, 39*, 472-480.

Schill, T., Toves, C., & Ramanaiah, N. (1980). Coping with loneliness and locus of control. *Psychological Reports, 47*, 1054.

Schill, T., Toves, C., & Ramanaiah, N. (1981). UCLA Loneliness Scale and effects of stress. *Psychological Reports, 49*(1), 257-258.

Schultz, N. R. & Moore, D. (1984). Loneliness: Correlates, attributions, and coping among older adults. *Personality and Social Psychology Bulletin, 10*(1), 67-77.

Schultz, B. J. & Saklofske, D. H. (1983). Relationship between social support and selected measures of psychological well-being. *Psychological Reports, 53* (3), 847-850.

Seligson, A. G. (1983). The presentation of loneliness as a separate diagnosis category and its disentanglement from depression. *Psychotherapy in Private Practice, 1*(3), 33-37.

Sermat, V. (1978). Sources of loneliness. *Essence, 2*(4), 271-276.

Solano, C. H. (1980). Two measures of loneliness: A comparison. *Psychological Reports, 46*, 23-28.

Solano, C. H., Batten, P. G., & Parish, E. A. (1982). Loneliness and patterns of self-disclosure. *Journal of Personality and Social Psychology, 43*(3), 524-531.

Townsend, P. (1957). *The family life of old people.* Glencoe, IL: The Free Press.

Weiss, R. (Ed.). (1973). *Loneliness: The experience of emotional and social isolation.* Cambridge, MA MIT Press.

Wheeler, L., Reis, H., & Nezlek, J. (1983). Loneliness, social interaction, and sex roles. *Journal of Personality and Social Psychology, 45*(4), 943-953.

Williams, J. G. & Solano, C. H. (1983). The social reality of feeling lonely: Friendship and reciprocation. *Personality and Social Psychology Bulletin, 9*(2), 237-242.

Wood, L. A. (1978a). Loneliness, social identity and social structure. *Essence, 2*(4), 259-270.

Wood, L. A. (1978b). Perspectives on Loneliness. *Essence, 2*(4), 199-201.

Woodward, J. C., Zabel, J., & Decosta, C. (1980). Loneliness and divorce. *Journal of Divorce, 4*(1), 73-82.

Cognitive Pastoral Psychotherapy With Religious Persons Experiencing Loneliness

Richard D. Parsons
Robert J. Wicks

ABSTRACT. While loneliness presents serious potential risk for emotional and physical disorders in the general population, for the "religious client" it can be particularly painful and destructive. The current essay presents a look at loneliness as experienced by the religious patient. In addition to discussing the potentially devastating effect that loneliness may have on the religious client, the authors provide a unique angle of vision for treatment of these patients. The model presented employs the theoretical framework of cognitive-behavioral psychotherapy but with a uniquely integrated pastoral dimension.

Relationships, as well as a resulting sense of connectedness and social bonding have long been considered to be essential to one's psychological well-being. However, cross-national surveys have demonstrated that the absence of such relationships is not only a painful experience but often a common one too. Estimates of the extent of loneliness have appeared to range from 11 to 26% cross-nationally, (Peplau, Russell, & Heim, 1979). These statistics are quite dramatic in their implication because persistent and sufficiently severe periods of loneliness have been correlated with depression (Bragg, 1979; Horowitz, French, & Anderson, 1982); alcohol use (Nerviano & Gross, 1976); physical illness (Lynch, 1977); and suicide (Diamant & Windholz, 1981).

Although loneliness presents an obvious serious potential risk for emotional and physical disorders in the general population, for the "religious client" it can be particularly painful and destructive. For Christians, relationships and being a part of "community" are usually not only viewed as being essential for psychological well-being, but are also seen as essential elements in living out the imperatives of Christian teaching, that is, "Quite simply, we can't approach salvation alone. The issue of God and

---

Mail requests for reprints to: Graduate Program in Pastoral Counseling, Neumann College, Aston, PA 19014.

community are inseparable'' (Wicks, in press). Therefore, the ''essentialness'' of relationship to both the psychological and spiritual health/well-being of the ''religious'' person serves to underscore the potentially devastating effect that a lack of relationship may have on this clientele.

The context of the problem of loneliness for religious patients, and the treatment modalities that are applicable with them, are not totally different from that of other persons experiencing such isolation and loneliness. However, religious patients bring with them elements of their unique cultural conditioning which make them uniquely vulnerable to the negative effects of loneliness and perhaps uniquely resistant to traditional modes of intervention.

The current essay presents a look at loneliness as experienced by the religious patient (for this paper the terminology will refer to Christians from so-called ''main line'' churches—i.e., Catholics, Presbyterians, Episcopalians, Lutherans, certain groups of Baptists, Methodists . . .). In addition, the authors attempt to provide a unique angle of vision for the treatment of these patients that not only employs the theoretical framework of cognitive-behavioral psychotherapy but also seeks to integrate a pastoral dimension to the treatment. It is felt that the results of such an integrated approach will result in the unique tailoring of treatment not only to the presenting problem but also to the population being served—namely, the person whose identity is strongly connected with, and formed by, a Christian religious tradition.

LONELINESS AND THE CHRISTIAN CULTURE

Loneliness is no stranger to most of us. We know it through direct personal experience and/or through our many professional and personal contacts. However, the transient, situational, or infrequent feeling of isolation, disengagement, or disenfranchisement experienced by most people at one time or another is *not* the loneliness to which we turn our attention. For the purpose of our discussion loneliness refers to ''an enduring condition of emotional distress that arises when a person feels that they are estranged from, misunderstood or rejected by others and/or lacks appropriate social partners for desired activities, particularly activities that provide a sense of social integration and opportunities for emotional intimacy'' (Rook, 1984, p. 1391).

Such a definition highlights the following three components which we feel are essential to understanding the nature of loneliness and the qualities that interact with the culture of religious patients to make them particularly vulnerable to its ill effects: (a) a culture of pain and denial; (b) a culture of ''community''; and (c) a culture of transcendence.

A Culture of Pain and Denial

As noted within the definition, loneliness is aversive. In this light, it is not the voluntary isolation of solitary prayer, or meditation. Quite often lonely religious patients will attempt to mask loneliness by referring to lonely periods as being their "self-imposed desire" to pray, meditate, or contemplate. "Knowing that we are all brothers/sisters in Christ and believing that we are called to 'accept' our individual crosses," religious persons may attempt to deny or rationalize the experience of loneliness. Yet, such denials are usually only partially effective and often eventually give way to vague feelings of dissatisfaction and/or symptomatology reflective of loneliness (e.g. depression, anger, alcoholism, etc.).

The clinician working with this population needs to be sensitive to these various attempts to deny loneliness or to justify it in terms of prayer, meditation, contemplation or self-sacrifice and personal denial. Working with the religious client requires that the clinician not only have professional sensitivity to detect the various clinical defenses presented, but also be theologically sophisticated enough to challenge its purported spiritual basis. First, unlike prayer, meditation and contemplation, loneliness is aversive. Secondly, most theologians agree that even solitary prayer to God involves key elements of community and relationship rather than disenfranchisment and loneliness. Steindl-Rast (1984), for instance says,

> Genuine prayer comes from the heart, from that realm of my being where I am one with all. It is never a private affair. Genuine prayer is all-inclusive. A great teacher of prayer in the Jewish tradition expressed this well: "When I prepare myself to say my prayers I unite myself with all who are closer to God than I am so that, through them, I may reach God. And I also unite myself with all who may be farther away from God than I am, so that, through me, they may reach God." Christian tradition calls this the communion of saints. (p. 52)

A Culture of "Community"

The belief generally held by most contemporary Christians is that we don't move toward God alone; we do it *together*. The trinitarian doctrine of God (three persons—Father, Son, and Holy Spirit—in one God) held by Catholics, the Eastern Orthodox church, Episcopalians, Lutherans, and others especially emphasizes the value and interest in relationships that Christians are *taught* to have. Holding on to this value and belief is essential to most Christians, even those experiencing loneliness. As such, when confronted with their own sense of isolation and disenfranchisement, lonely religious individuals will attempt to deny this experience of loneliness by "espousing" the belief of the kinship they have in the community of Christ.

Quite often religious individuals refuse to admit their loneliness noting that they are surrounded by their "brothers and sisters in Christ." The reality is that living and worshiping in common affords the opportunity for relationship but does not insure it. Further, loneliness cannot simply be equated with, nor narrowly limited to those situations in which one is socially alone. Claerbaut (1984), for example, expanded the definition of loneliness to include not only those situations in which we experience the absence of another individual but also the loneliness one feels when isolated from God (i.e., spiritual loneliness); the loneliness from self, which accompanies our own lack of a clear and certain identity (i.e., intrapsychic loneliness); and a special form of social loneliness referred to as "*loneliness-in*" which we experience when a relationship is present yet intimacy and real rootedness is absent.

Clearly, living and praying in "common," does not insure them protection against loneliness-in, intrapsychic loneliness, or spiritual loneliness. The clinician working with religious clients needs to accurately diagnosis both the type and source of loneliness experienced and not be misled by their reference to "available" community.

A Culture of Transcendence

The Christian person has been taught to seek a kingdom which is not only contained fully in the present world, but is of the world to come ("heaven"). Often the lonely Christian attempts to find justification in loneliness, and perhaps escape from its pain, by living life in the future using a transcendent God as an invisible friend who won't reject him or her. This has obvious positive and negative aspects. The potential positive outcome is that in chapel or alone in prayer lonely people might be able to get in touch with some of the positive points made in the *New Testament* about the intrinsic value of being human (i.e., everyone is made in the image and likeness of god) and thus feel accepted by a God who is portrayed in Jesus as a warm loving person. Yet, although such a belief is of potential value, there is a danger for such religious individuals in that they might be tempted to live only in the future and thus pervert the real world of present human relationships.

Under this form of denial and life of exclusion to all but the "distant sacred," the negative results of their prayer style may well outweigh the positive ones. For instance, the very solitary nature of some forms of prayer can actually encourage withdrawal and depression. Psychologically, not only do lonely persons set themselves up for problems of depression by lowering their activity level, but also when they seek to escape from loneliness by being away from people in prayer (which is a distortion of how religious denominations now view prayer), they run the risk of starting a vicious cycle in which they will become increasingly more uncomfortable with people and more alienated from themselves and the positive realistic feelings they should have about themselves. In addition to being psychosocially unhealthy, as was previously noted, such attempts to live in only the sacred world of a transcendent relationship with God is both theologically unsound and spiritually inappropriate.

To hold onto merely a *vertical* view of God—that is, someone who is only above and beyond us—is to deny the *horizontal* view that is also now commonly emphasized; in this view God should also be sought in each other. Accordingly, pastoral counselors traditionally point out to their clients the need to seek God in others and with others as well as in the transcendent, the invisible, or the intangibly mysterious.

Pastoral counselors recognize the powerful influence religious can have, for good or bad, on people. Since, religious individuals have most certainly been enculturated into a tradition of strong beliefs, the tradition, the values, the beliefs, can, if held maturely, provide a person with a raison d'être. However, as might be expected, these same beliefs, if immaturely misinterpreted and rigidly, uncritically held, can also provide bases for ongoing and unnecessary suffering.

Consequently the point being made is that when religious persons exhibit behaviors and feelings which reflect inappropriate attitudes that are encouraging loneliness they need to be addressed as *both* psychologically unsound *and* spiritually fallacious or immature. From this perspective, a pastoral cognitive-behavioral approach toward intervention appears especially well suited.

INTERVENTIONS—A COGNITIVE PASTORAL FOCUS

The Book of Proverbs notes, "As a man thinks, so he is." Such is also the basic premise of Cognitive-Behavioral Psychotherapy. From the cognitive perspective one's feelings are physiological responses to thoughts. That is, whenever one feels anything (emotionally), it is a result of a message, perhaps extremely brief and apparently automatic or instantaneous from one's thinking, interpreting (cognitive) system. A second major principle of this cognitive approach is that thoughts that lead to emotional turmoil and behavioral dysfunction nearly always contain gross distortions. Although such an interpretation might appear quite valid at the time, a closer, more objective analysis will reveal that it is irrational, dysfunctional, nonevidential—or quite simply wrong! (Parsons & Meyers, 1984, p. 90). The final basic principle of cognitive therapy is that one needs to be reeducated to identify one's dysfunctional, faulty beliefs in order to challenge these beliefs and to substitute more functional, rational ways of interpreting the reality one experiences.

As noted previously, the intervention strategies employed with religious individuals experiencing loneliness include those normally employed with a secular population. Thus the cognitive-behavioral techniques such as the use of Daily Mood Logs (Burns, 1984); Triple Column technique (Burns, 1980), and others can be employed by the pastoral, cognitive therapist. (The reader unfamiliar with these techniques is referred to the more elaborate detailing of these techniques and the principles of cognitive-behavioral psychotherapy found in a number of excellent basic texts of this approach (Beck, 1979; Burns, 1980; Ellis, 1975).

Even though these strategies are applicable to the religious person experiencing loneliness, the cognitive pastoral counselor/psychotherapist will use these principles with a special awareness of at least two additional aspects. One, there will be an eye to how religious values and beliefs are a source of support for the lonely person and how, conversely, a distortion of them might actually be contributing to or exacerbating the problem. And secondly, since pastoral therapists and counselors have their roots in a religious tradition, when they are cognitive in orientation they seek not only to eliminate cognitive distortions but also to do so in such a way so as to increase clarity and understanding which will form the basis for *metanoia* (conversion).

Thus, for the cognitive pastoral counselor/psychotherapist, being psychologically functional—healthy—is tantamount to being spiritually whole. Therefore, the goal in treatment is to clear the psychological "brush" (inappropriate thinking, cognitive distortions), especially as they are reflections of theological inaccuracies (i.e., "I'm so sinful that God couldn't love me—so how could anyone else?"; or "Loneliness is something God has willed on me . . . which I must simply endure"). In other words, there is an implicit/explicit belief that by increasing perceptual accuracy the person experiencing loneliness will then be in a better position to respond to God as a member of the church and thus begin to live a full, Christian life.

INTERVENTION—PROCESS

Theorists such as Ellis, Harper, Beck, and others may disagree with the particular strategies to employ in cognitive restructuring but most agree that the process requires attainment of three levels of "insight." First, the client must realize that feelings are created by his or her own thinking. Second, the connection between one's distorted beliefs and one's dysfunctional feelings needs to be made clear. Last is the realization that replacing the distorted belief and cognitive errors with more rational, functional ways of thinking will lead to more functional feelings and behaviors. The clinician working with the lonely religious client will find each of these *levels of insight* somewhat of a challenge to achieve.

Connecting Thoughts to Feelings (Insight #1)

As suggested, the first step in learning to reeducate and modify dysfunctional thinking is to truly accept the fact that feelings are a result of personal interpretation or "self-talk" occurring at any one moment. For example, if confronted by a man holding a gun most of us would feel a sense of fear, anxiety and perhaps panic. When asked to identify the source of this "feeling," we would most certainly identify the gun as the culprit! Regardless of the universality of this response—it is incorrect.

If the item—a gun—*caused* anxiety/fear/panic, then every gun (e.g., water pistols, collector's guns, stage props, etc.), when presented to any individual (e.g., an infant, a collector, an actor) would *cause* this reaction. Such is simply not the case.

On closer inspection we find that it is not the *event* of the gun that creates the reaction, but rather, it is our rapid, almost instantaneous *interpretation* of the situation as "life threatening." The point here is not to argue the justifiableness of such an interpretation but to simply make note that it is the interpretation, the belief, the self-talk which may appear as "Oh my God . . . . this is horrible"; or, "I am going to die . . . . I CAN'T STAND IT . . . WHY ME?" that causes the emotional reaction and not simply the event of being presented with a gun.

Assisting lonely religious individuals to gain this first insight is often quite difficult, because the feelings of despair, isolation, disenfranchisement have occurred for such a long period of time that the thoughts/beliefs tied to the feelings often appear almost unconsciously, or automatically. We have found that asking the client to keep a thought/feeling log or diary facilitates gaining an awareness of this thought-feeling connection. Specifically, clients will be asked to record in as much detail as possible the feelings and actions exhibited when they are experiencing loneliness. In addition to describing these feelings and actions, clients will be asked to describe the *events* surrounding this experience. What was happening to them? or, what were they doing? are questions they are asked to consider and to record. Finally, they are asked to attempt to separate the *facts* of the event (I was sitting at home watching TV) from the *belief/or interpretation* of the event (e.g., "I am really a worthless person—a real 'creep'—I am always alone doing dumb things like watching TV. If I were anybody I would be with a friend!"). This step is often difficult since the client has been interpreting, without reflection, for so long that "fact" and "opinion" appear intricately tied as one. Teaching the client to separate the facts from the opinion is an essential first step in the process of cognitive restructuring and may require direction and guidance from the therapist.

Recognition of (Insight #2) and Elimination of (Insight #3) Cognitive Distortions

The second step in the process of cognitive restructuring is to assist the client to begin to recognize those beliefs that are irrational, dysfunctional, or distorted. Teaching the client to identify automatic thoughts and to regard them as hypotheses to be tested rather than as facts, will reveal a number of unsupported, faulty beliefs. Thus the lonely client who insists on avoiding all occasions for social interaction—since "I always screw up in these situations and make a complete fool of myself," needs to be challenged to test this thought empirically. Reflecting on the number of times in which clients actually did "screw up" and did "make a fool" of themselves; asking them to experiment with this prediction by attending an affair and gathering data on the extent to which they made themself to "be fools" are exercises that will assist them to recognize that such is NOT ALWAYS the case and further that contrary to *being* fools, they have only *acted* in a foolish manner—a manner which is modifiable. Thus clients now have the data needed for debating this rigidly held, wrong (i.e., incorrect) belief and to begin to "problem solve" so as to be more adept at such social encounters.

Distortions of beliefs, or cognitive errors, can be created any time one overgeneralizes, personalizes, thinks only in terms of absolutes (black or white), or confuses fact with opinion. Under these conditions one's reaction (emotional and behavioral) will prove detrimental to goal attainment and thus must be considered dysfunctional. Thus the client who uses the occasion of watching TV to *believe* "it is clear that I am a worthless, un- lovable "creep" . . . who can do nothing better than isolate myself and stay at home watching TV, since clearly nobody could like me" will not only feel lonely and depressed, but will most likely remain in the house watching TV, thus fulfilling the prophecy! Further, when this belief is "put" to empirical test, it can be determined that labeling oneself as "unlovable" simply because there is no one to go out with is clearly an overgeneralization and personalization of the facts. Similarly, further in- spection of the facts will reveal that the belief that "I can do nothing bet- ter than . . ." is an inaccurate and unrealistic presentation of one's life in all-or-none/black and white term. These various forms of cognitive dis- tortions need to be identified for clients and they in turn need to learn how to recognize and challenge these distorted views of themselves and their world.

Elaborate and insightful discussion of typical cognitive distortions can be found in the works of Ellis (1962) and Burns (1980). The interested reader is referred to these texts for a more elaborate discussion of this topic. However, it has been our experience that there are two "generic" distortions that appear to be somewhat unique and commonplace to religious individuals experiencing loneliness and are thus presented in some detail below.

The "Catastrophe" of Being Alone

One of the generic beliefs most often exhibited by lonely individuals is that of believing that they *must* have a meaningful, intense relationship at all times and that its absence—aloneness—is *absolutely unbearable, unacceptable.* This unacceptability and unbearableness is exacerbated by the religious client's commitment to live and worship in the *community* of Christ.

The sense of urgency and absolute necessity of having a friend or of belonging creates a situation in which the lonely individual approaches each potential social encounter as "life or death situation." This intensity and sense of urgency is counterproductive to the development of a mutually satisfying, reciprocal relationship. Believing that one *must* have friends creates a sense of desperation that may lead a person to share too much too fast; or in turn to demand too much, too early in the relationship, rather than allowing the relationship to develop at the pace which is natural to it and to those involved.

For an individual to truly become facile at social skills, the urgency and sense of *absoluteness* or *mustness* needs to be surrendered. Although having a meaningful relationship is important and highly desirable, its absence is not an absolute, unbearable catastrophe and so, assisting clients to begin to enjoy social aloneness is a first step in assisting them to cope with their aloneness without creating a sense of overwhelming loneliness.

In working with religious clients experiencing loneliness, directing them to consider and reflect upon those moments in which aloneness was viewed as a time for reflection, integration, and prayer has been found to be useful. Reflecting on these "productive" periods of aloneness not only assists clients in challenging the fallacy of the belief that they absolutely can not tolerate being alone, but also encourages them to consider ways of productively, and positively, utilizing the time of aloneness. Further, assisting the religious client to relabel and redefine times of social isolation and aloneness as opportunities for solitude also proves effective in alleviating the pain of social isolation while facilitating the client's movement toward fuller understanding of, and communion with God, self, and the world.

One image that serves well in developing this concept is the image of Christ as he spent time alone in prayer and fellowship with the Father.

Clients are encouraged to conceive of themselves within a similar conceptual frame so as to employ solitude as an opportunity to gain a deeper knowledge and acceptance of themselves. With this understanding of self and fellowship with God comes a removal of the terror of being alone and a peace of knowing that being alone can be an enriching experience (Neale, 1984).

Solitude is a time when daily worries can be transcended; distance can be gained from the bombardment of stimulation and demands of the outside world; and one can get in touch with oneself and one's relationship with God. Directing religious persons to employ these moments of solitude creatively can be beneficial in that it provides the "data" from which to attack their irrational beliefs regarding the "unbearable," "catastrophic" nature of aloneness; and it further provides them with an expanded view of connectedness which includes: relationships with generations, things, the world, and most certainly God.

The essence then of de-catastrophizing aloneness is to have religious patients re-think and re-image this time to make it beneficial and rejuvenating. The danger in trying to do this, as was seen earlier in the paper, is that escapism and bonding solely to a vertical, transcendent God can take place. Clearly a balance is needed and the person must see that "beneficial aloneness with God" can be measured by the degree to which it includes self-love, self-esteem, and relatedness to others.

The Unworthy—Sinful Self

A second form of cognitive distortion quite often found among lonely religious clients is the belief that they are unworthy of a meaninful relationship. In such a case the belief is, "I am deserving of the pain of loneliness because of my own sinfulness."

The previous discussion regarding the utilization of aloneness to expand and nurture one's relationship with self, God, and the world through productive moments of solitude, was based on the premise that the lonely person is at least a light unto himself or herself. For those who find no light within . . . or who believe no light could ever exist, loneliness is all the more devastating and demands a major shift in one's own self-concept. Having such low self-esteem and strong belief in personal unworthiness not only inhibits any attempts to facilitate social interaction and relationship but exacerbates the already existing experience of aloneness into the devastation of loneliness.

Lonely persons are often unaware of their lack of self-esteem or, if they are aware of it, justify it by pointing to apparent faults in their character as evidence. Quite often they will point to limitations of the "conditions" of social worth, such as intelligence, status, good looks, the "in" clothes, cars, and so on as "evidence" of their unacceptability or unworthiness. Religious clients may extend these human conditions of acceptability to point to their intrinsic sinfulness and their obligation to be punished through such loneliness for their horrible, unforgivable sins.

The equation of conditions of life (job, money, and clothes) with the value of a human being, or the identification of oneself as unforgivable, is both psychologically and spiritually immature and unsupportable. Christian clients need to be directed to stop indulging in self-hate and punishment. Moving away from all-or-none thinking in which they see themselves as totally sinful or a total failure, if their performance is less than perfect, is essential for the ultimate elimination of these negative self-percepts. Similarly, falling into the error of labeling (i.e., wherein one attaches a negative label to oneself, instead of describing the error or shortcoming) can lead a person to conclude that he or she is a sinner and thus unworthy, unlovable, and undeserving of a relationship with others or with God. Again, such labeling is not only unsupported by the evidence of one's human reality (i.e., making one mistake does not make me a loser, but rather, a less than perfect human, which we all are) and is also theologically quite immature and inaccurate.

Religious clients exhibiting such an all-or-none labeling approach to their life can be assisted in their attack on these cognitive distortions by reviewing the message of the New Testament. The Gospels, especially the book of John, contain the message of the *unconditionality* of Christ's love.

Similarly, the review of the lives of "heroic Christians" (i.e., saints) can assist clients to redefine their own journey as simply that—a struggle, a process, a development task. The lonely Christians who think in terms of labeling and all-or-none concepts, refuse to recognize the process of their journey. They demand spiritual maturity, human and spiritual intimacy immediately, and interpret any sign of their absence as evidence of their ultimate and absolute failure. The lives of the saints and the story of the disciples show that growth is a *process,* a process which will be marked by setbacks and one which will be highlighted in Christian spirituality by the ever present love and support, through grace, of God.

We have found that the more clients view God rationally, as the all-loving being that Christian writings claim he is, the more clearly they come to accept their own humanity and the challenge of their own spiritual journey. When confronted by the rigid, negative self-concept and self-hating verbalization of the lonely Christians, we have found that pointing out to them they are no better or worse than all of humanity—a humanity whose salvation, Christians believe was bought with the blood of the son of God—creates a condition of some cognitive dissonance within them (i.e., How can I believe that God loved me so much that he would send his son to die for me—and all mankind—while at the same time believing that I am unlovable and unworthy of a meaningful human relationship?)

This form of congitive dissonance, confronting clients' own personal self-evaluation with their personal theological beliefs, creates the therapeutic tension needed to reshape the faulty self-percepts. A similar technique we have found useful in confronting and reshaping clients' dysfunctional thinking is to require them to extract from the Gospel phrases which highlight our value and acceptable quality to God and write them on a card to be read a number of prescribed times throughout the day. The use of these or other coverants, such as having clients repeat a favorite supportive, brief, New Testament quote, 20 times a day, again sets up a condition of cognitive dissonance in which their own perceived unacceptability is conflicted with by their reading or verbalization regarding Jesus' unconditional love.

The internalization of love frees the individual from the conditionality of human acceptance. Now, rather than neurotically chasing relationship as evidence for their own self-worth, clients can find peace within their sense of inner worth and adequacy. Once rid of these self-defeating attitudes and habits of putting themselves down, they can approach all social relationship with a relaxed sense of acceptability and value.

SUMMARY

Cognitive therapy has been demonstrated to have significant results with clients reporting symptoms of depression and loneliness. Given some of the unique aspects of religious clients' perception and experience of loneliness, there is a belief that the efficacy of cognitive treatment can be improved by integrating a *pastoral* dimension to the therapy of this population.

Although this can be done by involving a spiritual director/leader in the treatment, this paper has attempted to illustrate how a therapist versed in cognitive treatment who is also able to be sensitive and cognizant of the client's confession of faith (and its distortion which is a function of the depression/poor theology) can be especially helpful.

The theology which the client may ignore (i.e., God's love; self-acceptance because we are made in the image and likeness of God; life as a process which has suffering but doesn't seek it as an end in itself) can be brought into play as a basis for creation of a helpful, therapeutic dissonance and in turn a more appropriate cognitive set and self-esteem. Thus, it will set the stage for a more positive view of aloneness and a positive relaxed, accepting view of self which will in turn attract others rather than turn them away as depression and neediness tend to do.

REFERENCES

Beck, A.T., Rush, A.J., Shaw, B.F., & Emery, G. (1979). *Cognitive therapy of depression*. New York: Guildford Press.

Bragg, M.E. (1979). A comparative study of loneliness and depression. (Doctoral Dissertation, University of California, Los Angeles, *Dissertation Abstracts International, 39*, 79-13710.

Burns, D.D. (1980). *Feeling good*. New York: Morrow.

Burns, D.D. (1984). *Intimate conections* New York: Morrow.

Claerbaut, D. (1984). *Liberation from loneliness*. Wheaton, IL: Tyndale House Pub.

Diamant, L. & Windholz, G. (1982). Loneliness in college students: Some therapeutic considerations. *Journal of College Student Personnel. 22*, 515-522.

Ellis, A. (1962). *Reason and emotive psychotherapy*. New York: Lyle Stuart.

Ellis, A. & Harper, R.A. (1975). *A new guide to rational living*. N. Hollywood: Wilshire Book Co.

Horowtiz, L.M., French, R.S. & Anderson, C.A. (1982). The prototype of a lonely person. In L.A. Peplau & D. Perlman (Eds.). *Loneliness: A sourcebook of current theory, research and therapy* (pp. 183-205). New York: Wiley Interscience.

Leech, K. (1980). *True prayer*. New York: Harper & Row.

Lynch, J.J. (1977). *The broken heart: The medical consequences of loneliness in America*. New York: Basic Books.

Neale, R. (1984). *Loneliness, solitude and companionship*. Philadelphia: Westminster Press.

Nerviano, N.J. & Gross, W.F. (1976). Loneliness and locus of control for alcoholic males: Validity against Murray need and Cattell trait dimensions. *Journal of Clinical Psychology, 32*, 479-484.

Peplau, L.A., Russell, D., & Heim, M. (1979). The experience of loneliness. In I.H. Frieze, D. Bar-Tal, & J.S. Carroll (Eds.), *New approaches to social problems: Applications of attribution theory* (pp. 53-78). San Francisco, CA: Jossey-Bass.

Parsons, R.D. & Meyers, J. (1984). *Developing consultation skills*. San Francisco: Jossey-Bass.

Rook, K.S. (1984). Promoting social bonding. *American Psychologist. 39*, 1389-1407.

Steindl-Rast, D. (1984). *Gratefulness*. Mahwah, NJ: Paulist Press. (in press).

Wicks, R. *Availability: The problem and the gift*. Mahwah, NJ: Paulist Press.

Will You Be My Friend?
Group Psychotherapy With Lonely People

Brian D. Dufton

ABSTRACT. Group psychotherapy provides contexts for its participants to grapple with issues associated with the development of relationships. Given that loneliness can occur at any point in the course of a relationship, group psychotherapy may be of use in the alleviation of this condition. This article explores three phases of relationship development; that is, relationship initiation, deepening and termination. The article examines issues associated with each phase, first, suggesting how various factors may lead to loneliness in the course of a relationship and, then, noting how group psychotherapy can be utilized to address these isssues.

It is not good for a person to be alone. I will create another person to share life with the first (paraphrased from Genesis 2:18).

Loneliness has long been recognized to be a negative experience. It has been found to be consistently associated with aversive emotional states including depression, boredom, anxiety, marginality, and hostility (Perlman & Peplau, 1982). Loneliness has even been suggested as a potential cause in the development of cardiovascular disease (Lynch, 1976).

Loneliness is also highly pervasive. Yalom (1980) has called it the "common social malady." A high incidence of loneliness has been noted in psychiatric populations (Melzer, 1980), psychotherapy, encounter group, and T-group populations (Bradford, 1964; Goldman, 1955; Rogers, 1973) and in the general public. Bradburn (1969), for example, reported that 26% of people questioned in a survey had felt very lonely during the immediately preceding weeks.

One of the reasons loneliness is so common is that it can occur at any point in relationship development. For example, people who have trouble initiating relationships often experience loneliness either because of a lack of opportunities to be with others or because of a lack of social skills to enable them to make use of potential contacts (Rook & Peplau, 1982). Yet

Brian Dufton, Ph.D., received his doctorate in clinical psychology from the University of Manitoba in 1984. He is presently a member of the psychology department at Victoria General Hospital, 1278 Tower Road, Halifax, Nova Scotia, Canada B3H 2Y9. The author wants to express his appreciation to his colleague, Mark Olioff, for his helpful comments about the article.

other people experience loneliness in the context of already-existing relationships. Rook and Peplau have speculated that these people may feel lonely because of either restricted networks or a shallowness in the depth of their relationships. Finally, many people experience loneliness when relationships end. Whether it be death, divorce, separation, or even a move to a new location, people usually experience loneliness when those they care about are no longer there.

In summary, loneliness is an aversive, pervasive condition which can occur at any phase of relationships. Clearly, then, there is a need for treatment approaches having the goal of helping people deal with loneliness. In this article I will suggest how group psychotherapy may be used to that end. I will, first, describe how group therapy provides contexts for its participants to experience the issues of relationship initiation, development, and termination. I will, then, illustrate how this attribute of group therapy can be used to impact upon lonely patients during the course of a group. In particular, I will focus on group psychotherapy for patients who identify themselves as lonely.

GROUP PSYCHOTHERAPY

A number of writers have suggested that group psychotherapy allows for the development of a social microcosm of its participants (Bradford, 1964; Goldman, 1975; Yalom, 1975). In other words, psychotherapy groups reflect relationship patterns outside of the group. It has also been recognized that, once formed, groups evolve in somewhat predictable ways. They generally pass through three phases: They begin; they function as relatively stable units; and they end (Yalom, 1975). Insofar as groups proceed in this way, they serve not only as microcosms of existing relationships, but also as microcosms of the development of relationships. For example, in many respects, a beginning group reflects what occurs when people attempt to begin relationships, a developed group reflects what occurs when people have ongoing relationships, and a terminating group reflects what happens when relationships end. Thus, relationships both in and outside of therapy groups go through similar cycles.

It should be noted, however, that therapy groups also differ from other relationship contexts. Not only do they reflect habitual relationship patterns, they also provide opportunities for change that are rarely found elsewhere. In therapy groups, there is usually an active attempt to create an open, nonjudgmental, nurturant atmosphere (Rogers, 1973). For many group members, therefore, their participation in the group may be their first encounter with genuinely caring relationships. Such an encounter can greatly facilitate the giving and receiving of feedback. Learning is thus made more probable.

In summary, relationship patterns tend to be similar in and outside of groups. Psychotherapy groups, therefore, can provide contexts in which to focus on difficulties associated with loneliness in the course of relationships. The following section explores more explicitly how groups can be used to work toward the alleviation of loneliness during each three phases of relationship development.

RELATIONSHIP DEVELOPMENT

During each phase of relationship initiation, development, and termination people are faced with issues, the resolution of which can greatly influence how lonely and socially isolated they feel. During the remainder of this article I will focus on issues within each phase. First I will describe the issue and then I will outline how groups can be used to impact upon it.

Relationship Initiation

For the lonely, to be in contact with others is to be confronted with a host of possibilities. There are so many unknowns. They wonder, for example, whether these new contacts can grow into stable relationships. Or they may ask themselves what these relationships would do for them. Clearly, it can be an exciting time, a time of exploration. Yet the process of beginning relationships is often a difficult one. Many issues can cause fledgling relationships to stumble.

Self-Focus

When lonely people initiate relationships, their focus is often primarily on themselves. They wonder, for example, whether they are liked, or whether they will be rejected. A preoccupation with the self does not necessarily contribute to loneliness. It can, however, if an individual is so involved in self-evaluation that he or she misperceives (or ignores) how others are feeling. Eventually, self-absorption may alienate others.

Groups impact on self-preoccupation in a number of ways. Typically, the intensity of self-focus decreases as relationships develop. This is particularly the case if people feel that their own needs are being met. They then seem more able to orient themselves to the needs of others.

Nonetheless, some lonely people continue to be almost exclusively focused on themselves even while attempting to develop relationships. For them, specific feedback from others regarding excessive self-concern may be essential in order to encourage greater outer-directedness. As group participants learn that their manner of self-focusing can sometimes subvert the fulfillment of their relationship needs, rather than aid them, they may start to recognize such patterns as self-defeating. Moreover, the process of mutual caring, frequently evidenced in groups, can serve as a model of new ways of relating that are less excessively self-focused.

Aloneness

The person who feels lonely feels alone. Goldman (1955) has suggested that lonely people perceive themselves as minorities. They feel misunderstood, separate, and isolated (Perlman & Peplau, 1982).

Even just beginning a relationship, then, can start to decrease this sense of isolation. Group programs for the bereaved and for the maritally separated (Weiss, 1976) are based on this premise. Bradford (1964) has described "hand-clasping" efforts between group participants as they seek out others who might respond to them. Yalom (1976), furthermore, has listed the "disconfirmation of uniqueness" or the "experience of universality" as a curative factor particular to group therapy. For the lonely, a group can provide an opportunity to learn that others share their experience. Sometimes loneliness can then be normalized as a common life experience, rather than as one branding the lonely as misfits.

However, such experiences are not always sufficient to reduce aloneness. To illustrate, some participants may feel that their loneliness is in some way unique, either more or less severe than that of other group members, or that they have been lonely for either shorter or longer periods or that they are lonely for different reasons. It is instructive that some lonely people seem almost determined to maintain their sense of uniqueness even at the cost of maintaining loneliness. Participants can be encouraged to determine the accuracy of their perceptions by explicitly seeking ways in which others in the group are both similar and different.

Low Self-Esteem

Young (1982) has suggested that lonely people often have low self-concepts. They feel undesirable and unattractive. Their low self-esteem may be part of a larger cluster of beliefs and behaviors which ultimately inhibits the development of relationships (Peplau, Miceli, & Morasch, 1982; Young, 1982). For instance, people with low self-esteem are less likely to initiate contact with others. After all, they may reason, what would be the point in talking to someone if no one is going to be interested in them.

There are a number of ways in which group psychotherapy can impact upon such problems. One, groups give people the opportunity to be helpful to each other (Yalom, 1976). Frank (1964) has speculated that altruistic behavior can lead to a shift in self-perception from someone who is in need to someone who is able to be of benefit to others. Two, self-criticism is often particularly evident in groups and is, thus, made accessible to the interventions of others. Hollon and Shaw (1979) have suggested that "group sessions increase the likelihood that negative self-comparisons will be triggered" (p. 332). Such comparisons may take the form of feeling that others are less lonely or that others are progressing more quickly. Three, beginning group participants often seek acceptance and approval from others (Yalom, 1976). They may be, therefore, more open to the evaluations of others (Bion, 1959). Four, the group can be structured to provide opportunities for positive feedback from others or, at least, structured to avoid undue negative feedback. Five, groups provide opportunities for feedback from multiple sources, both the therapist and other participants, regarding the accuracy of self-perceptions. Feedback from other participants, moreover, may be particularly effective because, unlike the therapist, they are neither trained nor paid to be supportive. Thus, for instance, when a group member states that there is no point trying to talk to someone else because no one would want to talk to him or her, other members can counter the statement with powerful arguments that they are talking to them, they do want to talk to them, or that they would like to talk to them if only they would just stop sending messages that they are so unappealing.

In summary, lonely people have low self-esteem which group psychotherapy can help bolster. In particular, groups allow for positive feedback from other participants.

Competitiveness

Some people have difficulties starting relationships because of a strong need to compete and win. To these people, relationships may be seen as testing grounds to prove their dominance (Chesney, Eagleston, & Rosenman, 1981). Power seeking, however, can be self-defeating. People may gain power and even respect, but they lose opportunities for genuine closeness and caring. Others do not want to develop mutual relationships with those who seek to be superior, particularly if done in an aggressive manner.

Issues of dominance are particularly salient during the beginning phases of a psychotherapy group. Bids for power may be directed toward the therapist or toward other members (Bion, 1959). In the latter form, group participants may compete for the attention and good will of the group leader. Yalom (1976) has suggested that competition between participants is often evidenced by more frequent criticisms, a greater emphasis on "oughts" and "shoulds," and the establishment of a "pecking order."

The issue of power can be addressed through feedback from others that they feel alienated by a competitive quest for control. In addition, competitors can be encouraged to share about the sense of isolation engendered by their strivings. Perhaps the primary way of decreasing counterproductive, competitive behavior is through the development of cohesiveness and trust in the group. This issue will be further explored in a later section.

Withdrawal

Although aggressiveness may lead to loneliness, social withdrawal may do so even more directly. People who draw back from others are often in conflict; they want to have friends but they do not reach out. While bemoaning their isolation, they take no steps to initiate social contacts.

People may hesitate to relate to others for a number of reasons. Young (1982) has suggested that many lonely people experience substantial social anxiety. They find it hard to relax and to feel comfortable with others. Instead, they seem worried about how well they are performing. Other lonely people withdraw socially for fear of rejection. Such individuals mistrust others and are afraid that people will take advantage of them. People who have recently ended relationships are particularly apt to be afraid of further hurt or loss (Young, 1981). Finally, other lonely people withdraw from others out of habit; that is, they have gradually settled into a chronic pattern of isolation.

Group psychotherapy can impact upon withdrawal because being in a group does bring people into contact with one another. Yet, physical contact in itself does not end a pattern of withdrawal. Group members may be seen pulling their chairs away from others or picking a chair in a part of the room where no one else has yet sat down. In other words, withdrawal needs to be dealt with more explicitly.

Where withdrawal appears to be the result of anxiety, participation in the group may be of benefit, through the process of exposure and desensitization. In addition, cognitive-behavioral techniques, such as relaxation and distraction strategies, can be taught to reduce anxiety both in and outside of the group context. Where withdrawal appears to be the result of previous experiences of loss, it may be helpful for the group to explore why the previous relationships ended. Often the lonely individual may be overemphasizing either his or her role or that of the other person. Alternatively, the problem may have been less one of rejection and more one of geographical distance or the conflict of career aspirations (Young, 1981). Finally, where withdrawal has become an ingrained pattern, participants can be helped to become more aware of their behavior and encouraged to seek contact both in and outside of the group. Role-playing may often be helpful in this regard.

Social Awkwardness

Some lonely people have trouble initiating relationships because of a dearth of social skills. Young (1982) has noted that the socially awkward report being "ridiculed and rejected by others yet not know why" (p. 398).

Group psychotherapy recreates this common theme for the lonely. As Frank (1964) has noted, "early meetings are apt to be uneasy affairs" (p. 443): Group psychotherapy is usually a new experience for its participants. The latter frequently do not know what to do after the introductions. In the context of the beginning group, participants can find themselves having such thoughts as "It's all up to me," "Everybody must think I'm a bump on a log," and "This is awful." Exploring and altering these thoughts may be one step in helping group members cope with their sense of awkwardness. Moreover, as the participants learn how to behave in a group, they can be encouraged to restructure their perceptions so that they view other social situations as places where they need to learn new skills. Social awkwardness, thus, can become a challenge, a skills deficit, rather than a basis for a self-recrimination. Social skills training, furthermore, can be used to explicitly develop social skills for use outside of the group (Yalom, 1975; Young, 1982). Groups are ideal for lonely people to start practicing new social behaviors. In addition, the group gives opportunities to observe people with similar problems adopting more constructive interpersonal skills.

Summary

Lonely people typically experience a number of problems during relationship initiation. They are often self-focused; they may feel alone, have low self-esteem, be more concerned with dominance than with mutuality, tend to isolate themselves, and lack social skills. These issues also arise in group psychotherapy, particularly in the beginning group. Group psychotherapy can, thus, be used to impact upon these issues.

Relationship Development

As relationships develop, people begin to focus less on themselves and more on the interpersonal realm. Similarly, ongoing psychotherapy groups tend to become increasingly concerned with issues of intimacy and closeness. There is more active caring as well as greater self-disclosure (Yalom, 1975). Clearly, such experiences can be potentially very helpful for the lonely person. Nonetheless, there are a number of issues to be considered which can provoke loneliness at this stage of relationship development.

Mistrust

As noted earlier, lonely people fear rejection when initiating relation-ships. Even after taking the initial risk of starting relationships, many lonely people continue to hold back from deepening them because of their fear of being hurt. They may believe that if certain things were known about them then others would cease to be their friends. In fact, these fears can be even stronger after a relationship is established. Now, after all, the lonely person has even more to lose should he or she be rejected. Yet the reticence to deepen relationships by giving more of oneself to others can lead to further loneliness through the frustration and, ultimately, aliena-tion of other people who want to share at a deeper level. Furthermore, the mistrusting person may feel an emptiness because he or she realizes that others do not truly know him or her.

In the context of the developed group, lonely people are faced with similar conflicts. They now have begun relationships with other group members. In order to develop these further, they need to disclose more about themselves. Yet, they fear that if they do so, they will drive the other participants away from them.

There are a number of ways to help people approach this conflict con-structively. Mistrust can, for example, be normalized as an adaptive response to a potentially hazardous world (Nelzer, 1980). In this way, people can be granted permission not to trust. This is particularly impor-tant because many lonely people expect themselves to trust before they have had opportunities to test out the trustworthiness of others. These pa-tients need to be encouraged to view trust as a quality of relationships, a quality which develops gradually with every step taken (e.g., deciding to come to the group, disclosing about oneself). When lonely people accept that they can trust gradually, they seem able to take more risks.

Excessively High Expectations

People who are lonely frequently have excessively high expectations for relationships (Young, 1982). They seek for that group of people or, more often, that one special person who will make them feel fulfilled. To put this in another way, lonely people's attitude is often essentially passive. Having initiated relationships, they may feel a great lessening of distress. At long last, they will never be lonely again. Unfortunately, in-dividuals with such expectations will inevitably experience disappoint-ment! As with relationships in the past, the new relationships eventually are found to be deficient. Loneliness then reoccurs both because the rela-tionship does not meet expectations, and because the individual has not learned to approach everyday imperfections with an active, constructive attitude.

Curiously, rather than recognizing the inappropriateness of their standards, lonely people are more likely to begin the search anew elsewhere. In so doing, they fail to exert the effort needed to develop the relationships that they have started.

In a similar vein, inappropriate expectations may be evidenced by a number of behaviors in developed groups. For example, there may be an excessive focus on how others make the lonely person feel or on what others can do for him or her. In addition, there may be an increase in feelings of hurt or betraya!. People may feel let down by others. These feelings may be heightened further when, often as a result of passivity, a "special friend" has been "stolen away" by another group member.

There are several possible approaches to the person who expects that, having initiated relationships, he or she no longer needs to work at them. One way is the feedback of other group members that they expect active commitment on both sides of the relationship. Another way is to help make expectations more realistic, that is, perfect friends and partners do not exist and a search for such people typically results in loneliness. In other words, it is important for the participants to realize that the mere existence of relationships is not a panacea for loneliness. Even developed relationships in a psychotherapy group do not preclude feelings of loneliness.

Apartness

In the midst of caring relationships, people can feel themselves retreating. They can begin to feel separate from others. They may view relationships, previously perceived as positive, in a dispassionate, if not a cynical, manner. They may become spectators rather than players. A strong sense of apartness and consequent loneliness can then follow.

The above process evidences itself in a group in a number of ways. One is through the relatively sudden decrease in input from a group member. For example, an individual may fail to acknowledge his or her reactions to what is going on in the group. Bion (1959) has described such behaviors as defenses against involvement with others. It is as if people who retreat to their "apartness" have anxieties about making strong emotional commitments. They resist being what they perceive to be a passive unit swept up in the dynamics of the group.

Therapy can partly address this issue by emphasizing the interactive, interdependent nature of relationships. Group participants can be encouraged to focus both on their own bodily reactions to the behaviors of others and on the reactions of others to them. In this way, people can learn that they are never mere spectators.

Another way in which apartness can occur in a group is through the process of subgrouping, the formation of small groups or pairs within the larger group. Subgrouping is common in advanced groups (Yalom, 1975) and can be one way for an individual to resolve his or her concerns about involvement with others while maintaining some closeness. However, the latter has a price. People may miss opportunities to relate to more than one or two others. In addition, subgrouping places extra pressure on the relationships within that unit. At times, the subgroup may be expected to fulfill more needs than may be possible (reminiscent of excessive expectations for individual relationships). As these needs are left unmet, the subgroup participants may experience resentment toward each other. Again, loneliness may be elicited.

Subgrouping is a probable occurrence in most groups. One tact is to utilize it in a way that aids the development of other relationships. Subgrouping can be used as a model for working on particularly strong or valued relationships even while developing others which are perhaps less strong or less valued. In general, however, those who draw apart from others should be encouraged to develop potential relationships in a way and at a pace with which they can feel comfortable albeit not so comfortable that they take no risks.

Maladaptive Self-Disclosure

As relationships develop, people reveal more of themselves. Lonely people often find it difficult to achieve a balance in self-disclosure. They either tell too little or too much about themselves (Young, 1982). Either extreme can cause budding relationships to wither. When people tell too little, others can feel that the relationship is too one-sided. When people tell too much, others can feel overwhelmed, as if the relationship is proceeding too quickly. In either case, others may then withdraw.

Self-disclosure is an integral part of all group therapies, both feared and valued by its participants. Yalom (1975) has indicated that extremes in self-disclosure often occur in group psychotherapy. One goal of therapy, therefore, is to help people learn to reveal aspects of themselves at a rate which facilitates relationship development. In part, this can be done through feedback from other group members about their reactions to a member's self-disclosing style. It is important to add that the task of the group is not only to facilitate self-disclosure but also to give guidelines about its appropriateness in extra-group contexts. Again, role-play and practice can be very useful in this regard.

Conflict

Relationships often flounder because of conflict. People "just don't get along." Sometimes tensions develop even though people have seemed to initially "hit it off." Without the necessary skills to resolve conflict, people may drift apart, at least emotionally. Alternatively, they may tend to erupt in anger in such a way that potential resolution seems to be even less likely. Given that lonely people often lack conflict-resolution skills such as assertiveness (Young, 1981), their relationships are particularly at risk.

Conflict is inevitable in a group. Yalom (1975) has suggested that conflict can arise from the self-contempt of individual participants, distortions and misinterpretations of others, rivalry over particular roles in the group, or violations of group norms. In group psychotherapy it is possible to encourage people to deal with conflicts in ways that are at once more direct and less likely to end relationships prematurely. Yalom (1975), for example, has suggested that group participants can learn whether their anger is justified or whether it is expressed inappropriately. In part, this process can occur because of the push toward group cohesiveness. People are concerned with what others think of them. They are, thus, less likely to leave tensions unresolved. They are more likely to attempt to deal with them. The move toward conflict resolution can also be aided more directly. Through modeling, role-play, and practice, participants can be explicitly taught ways of expressing feelings of hurt and anger in a manner that is not self-defeating.

Summary

Starting a relationship is no guarantee against loneliness. Even though a relationship may be developing, it can falter because of mistrust, excessively high expectations, a strong sense of apartness, maladaptive self-disclosure, and unresolved conflict. These issues also occur in developed groups and therapy can be used a number of ways to help resolve them.

Relationship Termination

Loneliness does not always accompany the termination of relationships. Sometimes the strongest feeling is relief! Still, as relationships come to an end people do tend to experience feelings of loneliness.

Disinvestment

When relationships are coming to an end, people often begin to withdraw emotionally from those they will no longer be seeing (Bion, 1959). At times, this disinvestment may be premature and may even occur though there is still potential for relationship development. In so doing, people deny themselves opportunities to share feelings about the loss itself. Because disclosure about these issues may help in reducing the loneliness experienced upon separation, such individuals, if anything, increase the probability of feeling isolated.

Premature disinvestment also occurs in psychotherapy groups. Bion (1959) has noted that the "termination" of a group may often preceed its "end"; that is, people stop contributing to the group in order to protect themselves from the hurt of separation. As a result of the consequent barrenness, groups often decide to end earlier than planned.

One way of approaching premature disinvestment is to focus on feelings aroused by the impending termination. The therapist can draw attention to the feelings of loss as well as to the desire to avoid these feelings. In addition, while acknowledging the protective function of disinvestment, the group can be encouraged to continue working, that is, to continue the activities which predominated during the developed phase.

Denial

Another way in which people can respond to the ending of a relationship is to simply deny its occurrence. They may refuse to acknowledge any need to share feelings of loss or, indeed, that they experience such feelings at all. Instead, they seem to assume that the relationships will not change despite greatly altered circumstances (e.g., geographical distance, frequency of contact, unresolved conflict, or changed marital status). Such individuals may systematically avoid the expression of sadness or of grief.

In the short term, this tact actually may be quite helpful in avoiding loneliness. However, denial can also exacerbate feelings of loneliness. To illustrate, denial may prevent sharing and support between those who are to be separated. After all, if there is to be no loss, there is no reason to share about that. Should such individuals later experience loneliness, it may be even more severe than it might have been because the opportunities for mutual support are now either less available or completely absent. Furthermore, denial may increase loneliness by preventing the development of a new phase in the relationship, one of support for new relationships elsewhere. If people continue to invest all their energies into relationships no longer able to provide for their needs, they may miss developing relationships in their new situation.

Denial is also active when psychotherapy groups are ending. Participants may want the group to freeze in time as a place where no one or nothing changes (Bion, 1959). They may attempt to get together informally in order to maintain the group. Such meetings certainly have value and can be an appropriate way of moving relationships into a new phase. However, if group members hope to thereby recreate the therapy group, they will probably be disappointed: "It just doesn't seem the same."

As with premature disinvestment, denial can be approached by a focus on the feelings of loss and mourning. In this regard, it may be helpful again to give the participants permission to admit to such feelings. The group may be reminded of the impending termination by having the participants share their past experiences in the group (Bion, 1959). In doing so, participants can be encouraged to think of the group as evolving rather than as constant.

Disillusionment

Particularly for people who frequently experience loneliness, there is a tendency to respond to relationship termination with feelings of disillusionment. They may feel that relationships are ultimately too painful to try again, that is, "They always end anyway." Alternatively, they may feel that they will never have such relationships again and, therefore, they could never be as content again. Again, the disillusioned are less likely to initiate new relationships. Moreover, whatever few attempts at relationship initiation they do make are likely to be hampered both by their bitterness and by their desire to re-create old relationships. All in all, people who are disillusioned are likely to have more intense feelings of loneliness.

The ending group can provide a context in which disillusionment can flourish. Recall that for some lonely participants the group may have been their first taste of close relationships. They may, thus, respond with despair and anger at its passing.

In addition to focusing on the above feelings, people who feel disillusioned can be encouraged toward greater risk-taking outside of the group. Bion (1959) has stated that one of the tasks of the ending group is to support the transfer of learning to the extra-group context. This process can be facilitated by exploring possible hindrances to relationship development such as those outlined above. Participants need to be encouraged to recognize that new relationships will, in fact, be new. If participants have been gradually developing relationships outside of the group, these concerns may not be as strong. Nonetheless, when they do arise, perhaps the most helpful response is the question "Is it worth the risk to start again?".

Summary

It is common for people to respond with loneliness to the ending of relationships. This is particularly the case if the relationships have been perceived to be positive. For many, it is helpful to normalize such feelings as appropriate, if not adaptive. On the other hand, some people may respond to relationship termination in ways that could exacerbate feelings of loneliness. They may withdraw from others prematurely; they may deny the significance of the termination: or they may give up on relationships. All of these issues can be addressed in the context of the terminating group.

CONCLUDING COMMENTS

Group psychotherapy offers one avenue for helping people who experience loneliness. I have argued that, in particular, it provides a context for patients to experience and to explore a number of issues associated with loneliness in relationship initiation, development, and termination. Group psychotherapy can thus be utilized to help lonely people in a variety of ways, including reducing their social anxiety, developing greater self-acceptance, resolving interpersonal tension and conflict, and decreasing excessively high expectations to being more open about feelings of loss. As has been demonstrated, group therapy can accomplish these ends both through the expertise of the therapist as well as through the feedback, support, and modeling of the group patricipants.

I conclude with a quotation also paying tribute to the multifaceted nature of relationships:

Two are better than one, because they have a good reward for their toil. For if they fall, one will lift up the other; but woe to those who are alone when they fall and do not have another to lift them up. Again, if two lie together, they are warm, but how can one be warm alone? And though an enemy might prevail against one who is alone, two will withstand the enemy. A threefold cord is not quickly broken. (Ecclesiastes 4: 9-12).

REFERENCES

Bion, W. R. (1959). *Experiences in groups*. New York: Ballantine Books.

Bradford, L. P. (1964). Membership and the learning process. In L. P. Bradford, J. R. Gibb, & K. D. Brenne (Eds.), *T-group therapy and laboratory method* (pp. 190-215). New York: John Wiley & Sons.

Bradburn, N. (1969). *The structure of psychological well-being*. Chicago: Aldine.

Chesney, M. A., Eagleston, J. R., & Rosenman, R. H. (1981). Type A behavior: Assessment and intervention. In C. K. Prokop & L. A. Bradley (Eds.), *Medical psychology: Contributions to behavioral medicine* (pp. 19-36). New York: Academic Press.

Frank, J. D. (1964). Training and therapy. In L. P. Bradford, J. R. Gibb, & K. D. Brenne (Eds.), *T-group theory and laboratory method* (pp. 442-451). New York: John Wiley & Sons.

Goldman, G. D. (1955). Group psychotherapy and the lonely person in our changing times. *Group Psychotherapy*, 8, 247-253.

Hollon, S. D. & Shaw, B. F. (1979). Group cognitive therapy for depressed patients. In A. Beck, A. J. Rush, B. F. Shaw, & G. Emery. *Cognitive therapy of depression* (pp. 328-353). New York: Guilford Press.

Lynch, J. J. (1976). *The broken heart: The medical consequences of loneliness in America*. New York: Basic Books.

Melzer, M. (1979). Group treatment to combat loneliness and mistrust in chronic schizophrenics. *Hospital and Community Psychiatry*, 30, 18-20.

Peplau, L. A., Miceli, M., & Morasch, B. (1982). Loneliness and self-evaluation. In L. A. Peplau & D. Perlman (Eds.), *Loneliness: A sourcebook of current theory, research and therapy* (pp. 135-151). New York: Wiley-Interscience.

Perlman, D. & Peplau, L. A. (1982). Theoretical approaches to loneliness. In L. A. Peplau & D. Perlman (Eds.), *Loneliness: A sourcebook of current theory, research and therapy* (pp. 123-134). New York: Wiley-Interscience.

Rogers, C. R. (1973). *Carl Rogers on encounter groups.* New York: Harper & Row.

Rook, K. S. & Peplau, L. A. (1982). Perspectives on helping the lonely. In L. A. Peplau & D. Perlman (Eds.), *Loneliness: A sourcebook of current theory, research and therapy* (pp. 351-378). New York: Wiley-Interscience.

Weiss, R. S. (1976). Transition states and other stressful situations; Their nature and programs for their management. In G. Caplan & M. Killilea (Eds.), *Support systems and mutual help: Multidisciplinary explorations* (pp. 312-340). New York: Grune & Stratton.

Yalom, I. D. (1975). *The theory and practice of group psychotherapy.* New York: Basic Books.

Yalom, I. D. (1980). *Existential psychotherapy.* New York: Basic Books.

Young, J. E. (1981). Cognitive therapy and loneliness. In G. Emery, S. D. Hollon, & R. C. Bedrosian (Eds.), *New directions in cognitive therapy: A casebook* (pp. 139-159). New York: Guilford Press.

Young, J. E. (1982). Loneliness, depression and cognitive therapy: Theory and application. In L. A. Peplau & D. Perlman (Eds.), *Loneliness: A sourcebook of current theory, research and therapy* (pp. 379-405). New York: Wiley-Interscience.

Loneliness
and the Aging Client:
Psychotherapeutic Considerations

Samuel M. Natale

ABSTRACT. The article surveys the sociological and psychological themes and demographics that characterize the aging person. Loneliness as a manifestation of psychological and social development is examined. Individual and group modes of intervention to alleviate chronic loneliness among the aged are discussed and analyzed.

EXPERIENCE OF LONELINESS AND OLD AGE

Definition of Aging

Current literature supplies numerous definitions of aging. Since the process of aging may be conceived from various perspectives, the subsequent definition becomes a function of that particular view. The author favors a concept of aging consistent with the definition set forth by Birren and Renner (1977). They define aging as, "the regular behavior changes that occur in mature genetically representative organisms living under representative environmental conditions as they advance in chronological age" (p. 5).

We can further refine the definition by distinguishing between biological, psychological and social age (Birren & Renner, p. 5). Biological age is the individual's physical status in relation to his or her life expectancy. Psychological age refers to the adaptive behavioral capabilities of the individual in relation to other individuals. Social age deals with social roles the individual plays as well as social habits developed and must be judged in terms of societal expectations for the individual's age.

Changes in biological, psychological and social age are not necessarily parallel within the individuals nor are these patterns similar from individual to individual. Direction and rate of change may vary for each of

Samuel M. Natale, D. Phil. (Oxon.) is a graduate of the University of Oxford, England and the author of numerous books and articles. Dr. Natale is Professor at the Hagan School of Business, Iona College, New York and Research Fellow, Warborough Trust, Oxford, England. Mail requests for reprints to: 549 Colonial Road, Franklin Lakes, NJ 07417.

the three components. Decline or growth in one area is not necessarily associated with a proportional decline or growth in another area. It is therefore possible to experience a decline in physical status while simultaneously experiencing positive growth in psychological adaptive capabilities.

Factors Which Contribute to Loneliness in Old Age

Biological Correlates of Aging

As a biological process, aging is characterized by a decline in functioning which ultimately terminates with death. It is a "progressive loss of functional capacity after an organism has reached maturity" (Busse & Blazer, 1980 p. 5). There is a deterioration in major organs and systems; heart, lungs, kidneys, liver, nervous and digestive systems lose their former capabilities. The immune system weakens and the individual no longer resists disease with his/her previous strength. This results in "declines in mobility, energy, strength, and stress tolerance" (Yurick, Robb, Spier, & Ebert, 1980, p. 5).

How prevalent are physical limitations in the elderly compared with the total population? In 1980, there were 31.4 million individuals with an activity limitation due to chronic physical disorders (selected chronic conditions included heart conditions, arthritis and rheumatism, hypertension, impairment of back/spine, and impairment of lower back extremities and hips) (Statistical Abstract of the United States, 1982-83, p. 85). Of this total, 10.2 million were under 45 years of age, 10.4 million were between the ages of 45 and 64, and 10.8 million were 65 years of age or older. Although persons age 65 and older accounted for approximately 11% of the total population in 1980, they accounted for over one-third of all cases of activity limitation due to chronic illness.

Perhaps a more meaningful comparison is the percent of the population with no impairment. Of the total population, 85.6% are not limited by a physical condition while 54.8% of these 65 years and older enjoy this freedom. The contrast is heightened if we examine individuals 45 years and younger. In this case, a full 93.2% are free from the debilitating effects of physical impairment.

Although it is true that the majority of those 65 and over are in good health (if we define good health as the absence of an activity limitation), it is also true that the elderly experience substantially more restrictions based on poor health than the population in general. Logically, we can deduce that the increased isolation due to physical limitation contributes to the experience of loneliness in old age. Kivett (1978, 1979) provides support for this assumption in two separate studies. She classified 103 rural widows into three levels of loneliness: frequently lonely, sometimes lonely, and never lonely. She found that physical isolation as determined by self-perceived health and availability of transportation separated those who were frequently lonely from those who were never lonely. In the second study, Kivett classified 418 rural elderly into either high or low risks for loneliness. Poor vision and self-rated health were two of seven conditions which were associated with frequent loneliness. (The other conditions were widowhood, problems with transportation, frequent use of telephone, low participation in organized social activities, and being female.) Poor health has also been found to account for conditions related to loneliness. Mussen, Honzik, and Eichorn (1982) found that poor health was associated with a lack of life satisfaction in elderly men. Likewise, Markides and Martin (1979) and Beck (1982) found life satisfaction and happiness to be strongly associated with good health in the elderly.

Developmental Views of Aging

As early as 1933, Jung saw the later half of life as a process of turning inward toward the self. To deal with one's impending death one must, to some degree, remove oneself from the world. In introspection one develops a philosophical or religious view of life and death (p. 55).

Erikson views the life cycle as a series of stages which have specific goals (p. 87). In the last stage, the individual must attain ego integrity by turning inward, examining one's life, and accepting it as it has been lived. If the individual cannot develop a sense of integrity from past accomplishments, but instead focuses on past mistakes and missed opportunities, despair results. Perhaps the most extensive work on the theme of turning inward has been proposed by Cumming and Henry (1961). Based on their study of a health cross-section of the elderly in Kansas City, they introduced a concept which has been known as disengagement. Disengagement theory holds that the elderly person withdraws and detaches himself or herself, gradually reducing contacts and involvements with the larger society. This is seen as a natural, adaptive process that is necessary because of the elderly individual's impending death. Cumming and Henry viewed disengagement as a necessity for successful adaptation to old age.

Although subsequent research does not substantiate the disengagement process as a healthy adaptation to aging, it is difficult to point to a cause and effect relationship (Larson 1978, p. 109). In other words, did the elderly turn inward to an effort to examine their life and values or were they forced into passivity and isolation because of poor health? We might conclude that those who choose a contemplative life-style would be well adjusted while those who involuntarily withdrew would not. Unfortunately, most research to date has not separated the effects of these intervening variables.

Owens (1981) feels that turning inward can indeed be beneficial in old age (p. 113). She sees an absence of wholeness, expressed in the lack of integration of left and right hemispheres of the brain, as a cause of many difficulties experienced in old age. She proposes the use of meditation as a means by which attainment of wholeness is possible. Meditation allows the activation of previously buried virtues. It enables the individual to use these resources to deal with the problems of aging. By the process of meditative exploration, the "true self" is found. This true self paves the way for the "moment of becoming" when the individual experiences a oneness with the universe. Owens feels that meditators can find companionship in their awakened selves and in their experience of oneness with the universe. This companionship is a powerful aid in dealing with loneliness.

She states that meditation ". . . transforms the whole hierarchy of values from the seen to the unseen. The chief riches valued by followers of the Eternal Way are inner wealth: certitude, courage, creativity, honesty, love, desire to serve others, selflessness, purity and joy" (p. 113). We can conclude therefore, that turning inward can be beneficial in dealing with problems of old age if it is utilized as a development of psychological resources. Removing oneself for the purposes of solitary contemplation, be it expressed as meditation or as prayer, can be a positive experience in old age. If the individual uncovers previously obscured inner resources, withdrawal can be comforting and productive.

The Role of Sociocultural Factors

Despite an increased awareness and acceptance of the aging process in recent years, ageism continues to exist in American society and is one factor contributing to the experience of loneliness in old age (Butler, 1969, p. 243). Alex Comfort (1980) speaks of the cultural problem termed gerontophobia. He states that, "unique to our culture is its rejection of the old, their exclusion from work and their accustomed social space, their premature burial as 'unpeople', and a rich and erroneous folklore of mental decline, infirmity, asexuality, ineducability, and the normality of causeless mental disorders in the old" (p. 2).

Changes in chronological age are typically accompanied by changes in social roles. At earlier points in the life cycle, loss of one role is usually substituted by another. For example, a college student will, upon graduation, lose the role of "student." However, it is likely that this role will be replaced with "employee." A young couple may no longer consider themselves "newlyweds" after the birth of their first child. They have however, now acquired a new role: that of parents. The difference between this type of situation and that of the elderly revolves around the issue of replacement.

When an elderly person retires, the work role is frequently not replaced with another job. Loss of employment is often accompanied by a loss in economic security and social status. One can no longer define oneself as an employee of XYZ Company. Contributing to loneliness may be a loss of contact with co-workers and friends. Unlike the young person who has the opportunity to replace this job with another, the elderly individual's role loss is permanent.

Another frequent role change experienced by the elderly is that of marital status. With increasing age, the loss of spouse through death becomes more probable. The widowed individual loses much more than an identity; he or she loses a lifelong partner, a companion, and a primary source of psychological support. Because of lack of time and opportunity, remarriage (replacement) becomes less likely. This type of unreplaced role loss is not universal nor has it always been the case.

Gutmann (1980) feels that certain types of societies are more suited to supporting the mental health of the elderly than others. According to Gutmann, the small, face to face, traditional folk society comes closest to providing optimal support for the elderly. Hareven (1978) also supports this general view. She feels that the negative image of old age and consequent isolation of the elderly from the mainstream of society are a function of increasing segragation of different life stages in modern American society. She points out that, "The absence of dramatic transitions to adult life allowed a more intensive interaction among different age groups within the family and the community, thus providing a greater sense of community and interdependence among people at various stages in the life course" (p. 208).

Although both Gutmann and Hareven concur on the type of social structure most supportive of the elderly, Gutmann proposes a somewhat different perspective on causation. He states:

> There appears to be an assured, organic linkage—a "deep structure"—that bond the older traditional persons and the sacred systems of their culture as these are represented in theology, in myth, and in ritual. This special bonding between the sacred and the geriatric leads to traditional gerontocracy, to special privilege and esteem for the aged, based on their special access to spiritual resources. (p. 433)

A loss of isolation causes a redistribution of power within the previously insulated society. The introduction of new ideas weakens the strength of the old. Economic power is now accessible from sources other than familial holdings. The power base shifts from within the culture to an outside source. Gutmann distinguishes between urbanization and modernization, stating that the former is not necessarily a product of the latter. In modernization, a different culture is accepted as better than that of the present one. If however, both rural and urban areas are part of the same social evolution, harmony of process is achieved. Before their contact with the West, Oriental cities preserved traditional values, rituals, and practices. It is therefore theoretically possible to maintain a supportive social structure for the elderly in modern urban society.

Gutmann proposes a creative solution to a very difficult problem. He points out that certain secular professions—for example law, medicine, and academia—might create the essence of the earlier religious function of the elderly. Appointing older practitioners to represent the ethical standards of the profession would effectively recreate the sacred status of the aged.

These professions resemble folk society by sharing a strong distinction between the sacred and the secular. The younger members would address the routine norms of practice while the elderly would address the moral issues. The elder, no longer motivated by self-interest in building a career, can be a more objective spokesperson for the ethical position. The elder's function would therefore be of value to society, and also supportive of the social status and mental health of the aged in modern society.

Situational Factors and Loneliness in Old Age

Retirement and Income

Although one might expect retirement to be correlated with loneliness and an overall detrimental effect in old age, this is not always the case. There are several intermediate and interconnected conditions that determine whether or not retirement has an adverse effect on the elderly.

Income is a significant determinant of the evaluation of retirement. Beck (1982) found that lower income was one of the main determinants in a negative evaluation of retirement. In March of 1982 the median annual income for all persons in the United States was $19,074.17. For those aged 65 and over, the median annual income was only $9,903.18. Only 20% of the elderly have annual income under $5,000 (Statistical Abstracts 82-83).

To the extent that low income reduces opportunities, status, and the overall quality of life, and to the extent that retirement results in a reduction in income, we can conclude that retirement has an adverse effect on the elderly.

The state of the elderly individual's health is another significant factor in the overall evaluation of retirement (Beck, 1982). Poor health is associated with a negative evaluation of retirement and, as discussed previously, limits mobility and opportunities.

A significant determinant of good adjustment to retirement, and the area which offers the most constructive avenues for possible change, is the extent to which the retired individual has substitute satisfactions available (Botwinick, 1978, p. 82). Meaningful volunteer work for the elderly has been proposed as one such substitute. Hunter and Linn (1980-1981) compared retired elderly volunteers with non-volunteers and found that volunteers had a significantly higher degree of life satisfaction, a stronger will to live, and fewer psychologically maladaptive symptoms (depression, anxiety, somatization). Palmore (1980) proposes that religious institutions (churches, synagogues) may offer a fruitful alternative for previous work role. Religious institutions are a logical place where elders can assume meaningful roles within the organization because they are the community institutions to which elders most frequently belong. Because, in all likelihood, the elderly have been lifelong members, a sense of continuity is provided as well (p. 236).

Living Situation

Although living alone does not necessarily imply a higher level of loneliness it seems logical that physical aloneness might predispose the individual to a higher risk of loneliness. The elderly are more likely than any other age group to reside by themselves. In 1981, persons 65 years or older comprised 39.5% of all individuals living alone (Statistical Abstracts 82-83). Cohen (1980) points out that living alone reduces the availability of an immediate source of social support and interaction. The lack of this social support is detrimental to healthy psychological adjustment.

The areas in which older individuals tend to reside further exacerbates possible loneliness. The elderly live in rural or urban settings more frequently than younger individuals do (Hendricks & Hendricks, 1977). In rural settings, people become isolated by physical distance. Fear of crime may impose a need for self-imposed isolation on the urban elderly.

The author has excluded the institutionalized elderly from the discussion up to this point because, contrary to popular belief, only a small portion of the elderly reside in nursing homes and similar institutions (Ingram, 1977, pp. 303-308). Here the possibility for experiencing loneliness as a function of living situation increases. Dudley and Hillery (1977) report that alienation and lack of freedom are more frequent for nursing-home residents than for any other type of institutional residents.

Death of Spouse and Peers

It is an undisputable fact that the probability of loss of a spouse and peers increases as an individual advances in years. Although both sexes are more likely to be widowed as they age, women are much more likely to experience the loss of a spouse through death than men. In 1981, the percent of males widowed was as follows: age 55-64—4.1%, age 65-74—8.2%, age 75 and over—22.1%. For women the respective percentages were 18.4%, 40.1%, and 68.2% (Statistical Abstract).

The most common psychological disorder in old age is depression (Comfort, 1980). Depression is linked with loss, including the loss of a significant other (Steur, 1982). Loss of a spouse through death increases the risk of mortality for the surviving spouse (Epstein et al., 1975; Payne, 1975). Paul Tillich (1980) states that the loneliness felt as a result of separation or death is the most widespread type of loneliness. The feeling of loss is heightened because the intimacy, contact, and communication experienced with these individuals helped us forget that we are alone. It is to this type of loneliness that formal religion most frequently addresses itself. The Judeo-Christian tradition offers solace to the bereaved with the hope for Eternal Life. The loss and loneliness experienced as a result of death can be viewed as temporary. Both the Hebrew and Christian Scriptures reassure the reader of the worth of the human soul and convey the certitude of a life after death.

An alternate approach to the problems of death and loneliness is offered in Zen Buddhism (Keefer, 1947). Both the experience of loneliness and the fear of death are results of the illusion of "self." The "self" is merely a collection of beliefs, tastes, and desires and can be abandoned. Experience itself is value neutral although characterized by duality. Life and death, therefore, are simply dualities of one type of experience. The same holds true for loneliness and a sense of belonging. According to Zen, these dualities may be experienced as painful or joyous at any particular point in time but contain no intrinsic value in and of themselves. They are simply part of the natural complexity of human existence.

Productive Solutions to the Problem of Loneliness in Old Age

Types and Variations of Loneliness

It is helpful to realize that loneliness is not a single entity and that productive solutions to the problem of loneliness will depend on the type of loneliness being addressed.

A general definition of loneliness is proposed by Jacob Landau (1980). He states that "loneliness means to feel our apartness, or inability to bridge the gaps that exist or may arise between ourselves and others" (p. 498). Keefer (1980) puts forth the following definition of loneliness: "I think, rather, that feelings of loneliness occur only when a person experiences deprivation of emotional gratification, and the deprivation is perceived to result from the inability of the lonely one to communicate his or her need to another being or other things" (p. 426).

Finally, an excellent general definition of loneliness is also proposed by

Rubenstein and Shaver (1982). To them, "loneliness warns us that important psychological needs are going unmet. Loneliness is a healthy hunger for intimacy and community—a natural sign that we are lacking companionship, closeness, and a meaningful place in the world" (p. 2).

Landau further differentiates the concept of loneliness into social and individual loneliness. Of the two types of loneliness, social loneliness, according to Landau, is inherently soluble. Although it is experienced on an individual psychological level, it stems from social conditions and transactions. Individual loneliness however, is more difficult to conquer. It can be termed existential and can only be overcome by a recovery of lost cosmic interconnectedness.

These two conceptions of loneliness are not mutually exclusive. It is often difficult to draw the line between one type of loneliness and the other. However, in the most elementary sense, we can conceive solutions to social loneliness by a movement toward others while existential loneliness must first be conquered by a movement toward the self. After the self has been discovered we find that movement toward others naturally follows. The distinction between the two types of loneliness might very well explain the often contradictory results of research in the area. Although the bulk of research equates healthy adjustment in old age to be highly correlated with the level of social interaction, this does not necessarily disprove the earlier developmental theories of Jung (1933), Erikson (1959), or Cumming and Henry (1961) who equate satisfactory adjustment in old age with a turning inward toward the self. It is quite possible that we are dealing with two types or levels of adjustment. The differentiation between healthy introspection and pathological withdrawal was not made or measured.

This leads us to a rather paradoxical distinction between loneliness and solitude. Although loneliness is often experienced as a consequence of isolation it is not necessarily equated with the state of being alone. It also follows that one may feel lonely despite social interaction. According to Rubenstein and Shaver, "solitude is a kind of positive aloneness. And, paradoxically, solitude can be a corrective for prolonged loneliness" (p. 15). How can solitude be a productive solution to the problem of loneliness? Rubenstein and Shaver feel it is because of the relationship between active solitude and intimacy. They state, "in solitude we are intimate with ourselves in a way that enhances our intimacy with other people" (p. 176).

The concept of aging proposed by Birren and Renner (1977) was described earlier. This definition focused on changes experienced by the individual and was not limited to deterioration or decline. The elderly can experience both growth and decline in various areas of functioning. The aged have the capacity for growth and adaptation in the spiritual psychological area even though physical functioning may decline. This concept of aging is surprisingly similar to the Christian view of adulthood (Bouwsma, 1978, p. 55).

This view lacks an interest in chronological differences among individuals: The Christian life is perceived as a process of growth and all people are equal to the extent that they are growing spiritually or stagnating. The Christian way of life implies the experience of challenge and struggle. The Christian adult is not to avoid these challenges but rather to experience them and to grow spiritually as a result. Possibilities for growth are indefinite and the process continual. The special problems of old age can therefore be viewed as opportunities for further spiritual and psychological growth.

Self-Concept and Healthy Adjustment to Aging

"Self-concept refers to the cognitive aspects of self-perception and consists of individuals' perceptions of themselves" (George, 1980, p. 14). It relates to self-esteem, which "refers to the affective and evaluative aspects of self-perception and consists of judgments made about the self as an object."

A comprehensive survey of individuals over 65 was conducted by Harris and Associates (1975). It was found that 56% of those over 65 years of age felt they were as happy now as when they were younger. This suggests that the majority of the elderly have a positive self-concept. However, a large percentage may not feel this way. One must realize that self-concept is a continuous process. The individual tends to maintain a self-concept consistent with that which was held in earlier years (Brubaker & Powers, 1976). In other words, if the individual had a positive self-concept before old age, it is likely that this positive self-concept will be maintained. The same holds true for a negative self-concept.

Many of the changes which accompany old age have been discussed. Several offer a potentially detrimental effect on self-concept. Failing health; a reduction in income; loss of friends, family, and work-role—all of these changes threaten a positive self-concept. Yet many elderly can and do maintain a positive self-concept. Research has shown that certain conditions correlate with a positive adjustment to aging.

One of these correlates is the maintenance of an inner-directedness. Mancini (1980-1981) has shown that locus of control was positively correlated with higher life satisfaction. This association was maintained even when controlling for other variables such as income and self-rated health. Reid et al. (1977) also confirm this association. They found that those with a negative self-concept tended to be less in control and less happy than those with a positive self-concept. Gutmann (1978) conducted an exploratory study of 410 elderly subjects and he too confirmed the link between control and a positive self-concept. He found that action taking was strongly associated wih well-being in the aged.

The relationship between these findings and religious experience is clear. To the extent that prayer, solitude, or contemplation increases an awareness of self and promotes a greater degree of inner-directedness, it will be related to a positive self-concept in old age. Those with a positive self-concept are much less likely to be lonely than those with a negative self-concept (Anderson et al., 1983).

Research overwhelmingly supports the view that social involvement enhances the maintenance of a positive self-concept, is associated with good adjustment to old age, and is negatively related to loneliness. Lopata (1980) interviewed over 1000 widows in the metropolitan Chicago area and found that the lonely lack social supports. They are also angry people who cannot draw emotional support from others. Rubenstein and Shaver (1982) analyzed approximately 30,000 surveys in their study of loneliness. They conclude that "The only lasting remedies for loneliness are mutual affection and participation in a genuine community" (p. 18). Mc-Clelland (1982) points to the importance of social interaction in the maintenance of a strong, positive, self-concept and stresses that continued interaction is necessary to sustain it.

Snow and Crapo (1982) further confirm this association in their study of emotional bondedness in elderly medical patients. Emotional bondedness includes the sense that one receives support from another, the sense that there is mutual sharing with another, and the sharing of positive feelings with another. They studied over 200 aged ambulatory medical patients and conclude that emotional bondedness is positively related to health and subjective well-being.

On both personal and institutional levels, religious experience can foster a sense of community and belonging that counters loneliness and a negative self-concept (Staser & Staser, 1976). In fact, Kalsh (1979) feels the absence of substantial numbers of elderly in traditional counseling settings may be explained by their utilization of the church for social and emotional support. He advocates the expansion of religious support services for the aged.

Perhaps the most significant problem in old age is that of loss. Loss frequently results in lowered self-esteem (Lazarus, 1980). Physical and interpersonal losses have been linked with psychopathology in the elderly (Blum & Tross, p. 148). The key to successful adaptation to loss appears to lie in the individual's ability to replace that loss (Wigdor, p. 257). On an individual level, religion may offer explanations for loss of comfort which lessen the degree and impact of loss. It may provide meaning to this painful experience. The teachings of most formal religions support altruism. Rubenstein and Shaver (1982) state that, "Altruism is an effective way out of loneliness . . . Forget yourself for a while and attempt to help others. Paradoxically, you may solve your own problem in the process'' (p. 184).

Rubenstein and Shaver highlight an essential ingredient in replacing loss—reaching out to others. As mentioned previously, formal religious institutions are the community institution to which elderly individuals most frequently belong. They provide an ideal medium by which the aged can reach out to others and replace losses with new social contacts. By becoming actively involved in the church, they can assume meaningful roles to replace other, lost roles (work roles, social roles, etc.). In the process of reaching out to help others the elderly can ultimately help themselves.

Psychotherapeutic Treatment of Loneliness in the Older Adult

We have explored the relevant background information necessary for anyone who intends to work with the older client. We now turn our attention to the direct issue of treatment.

As in all psychotherapy, it is essential to examine the beliefs of the therapist as well as of the client. For effective growth and development on the part of the client to take place, it is imperative that the therapist acknowledge that there is a possiblity of development and improvement throughout the *entire* life cycle—including old age. Too frequently the effective treatment of older adults is hampered by individuals ignorant of gerontology who believe that any intervention for the older adult is useless because the individuals are at the end of the life cycle. Other biases may include the more veiled disinterest on the part of therapists because client who is old is seen as too "set in their ways"—a euphemism for rigidity, as well as "old fashioned" and un-psychological-minded.

There are specific technical and human skills which must be developed by the therapist involved with older adults, it is true. However, many of the criticisms leveled against the older adult are simple stereotyped social thinking—in short, a varied form of age discrimination.

The problem is often compounded by the fact that older clients often evoke negative countertransference reactions from therapists as well as making them feel uncomfortable, since the therapists must face the reality of the mortality of everyone—including themselves!

Loneliness is inescapable in old age, at least in some form. The older adult faces separation from valued roles as well as from loved family and spouses. At the same time these losses are wrenching the person, his or her social circle is getting smaller and smaller. The old person is also often having to face chronic illnesses and diminished energies.

The loneliness which is inevitable often manifests itself in the treatment of the older adult as a "hunger" on the client's part to reminisce. The therapist must be prepared for a greater amount of sharing of memories and a "talkiness" which would more quickly be interpreted as resistance in a younger client. The facts are, however, that the older adult may have so few contacts that the therapist's attentive listening is *the* critical ingredient in at least alleviating some of the pain of loneliness.

In the treatment of the older adult, the therapist must encourage a review of the person's life and provide the client with an opportunity to expiate past offenses—even if the persons involved are dead. Many less experienced therapists seem to suggest that "nothing can be done" because the people involved are dead. However, the absence of some of the parties from the current human drama does not render them insignificant to the client. It is crucial that the therapist enable clients to survey both the things they have done and the things left undone as they summarize much of their life. The encouragement and listening to the clients have demonstrably reduced the sense of isolation and loneliness in itself and has enabled them to "frame" their life in terms of the past achievements as well as the facing of the inevitability of death.

Old age does not happen all at once, however. It is crucial that the therapist determine whether the loneliness of the client is situational (arising from the death of friends, retirement, loss of spouse, etc.) or chronic, that is, the result of a lifelong deficit of social skills.

Social-skills behavioral training can be used as effectively with older adults as with any other age group, though the therapist must be sensitive to the cohort values that characterize the specific individuals.

If the loneliness is predominantly situational, the therapist may provide a transitional link for the client as the person reconnects to other friends, social groups, church, and so on. The reaching out of the lonely older adult can be responded to with directness and interest.

If, however, the loneliness is chronic the therapist *must* become involved in psychotherapy on three levels, *simultaneously*. The therapist must get the client involved in (1) *behavioral/cognitive* changes; (2) *insight* to enable the client to detemine the psychodynamics and background understanding so that current deficits can be remedied, and, finally, (3) *support*—to encourage further exploration. The traditional separation of these therapeutic functions so common in general treatment are not acceptable in the treatment of loneliness in older people. The therapist will have to take his or her cue for which intervention to begin with from both the client's personality (is the person active or passive?) as well as from whatever issues are immediately emergent.

If the therapist is able, it is most helpful to visit the older person in his or her living situation (private apartment, home, convalescent center, etc.) to assess the effect of various living settings on the person's affect. This is particularly useful when an individual is in some kind of group living and still experiences genuine isolation and loneliness. The therapist can quite directly assess the impact of ailing individuals all living separate lives in common. Often the only stirring topic is one's current illnesses and discomfitures. Clearly, it is useful for an already sad/depressed individual to distance oneself from such a situation, however, in the case of the aging person, to distance oneself from this group is to impose very real isolation. Unless the therapist can help these individuals connect with some other, more positive experiences, it may be necessary to conduct the therapy wholly within the limitations of the person's life. Sometimes, naively, less experienced therapists (and older ones as well) suggest that individuals should simply "detach" from the negative people around them. This can be deadly advice, especially for those in custodial care. Ironically, *some* relationship is generally better than no relationship.

The suggestion that the therapist visit with older clients in their home is not one suggested lightly. In fact, if the therapist is not willing to make "house calls" I believe treatment should *not* be undertaken. Visiting individuals where they live enables the therapist to assess the social and economic world of the client. This kind of intimate contact with clients and their daily living environment necessitates that the therapist become involved in wholistic treatment that involves a capacity to go beyond the often artificial separations which divide the professions and require that the therapist become *actively* involved in helping the client seek appropriate housing, if necessary and to be a co-worker with the client's physician. Involvement with social services and nutritionists is an often necessary adjunct as well.

The most frequently recounted fears of older clients involve a fear of both poverty and of loneliness. In responding to the client's fear of loneliness, it is crucial that, as in any other treatment, the therapist acknowledge the *validity* of the concern and then begin involving the client in expanding their repertoire of interests, skills, activities, etc. If the client's world is however limited by a wheel chair or hospital bed, it will require more creativity and energy for the therapist to involve the client who is lonely. However, the creative use of intellectual interests (talking books, etc.) as well as pets have been found to be highly effective in the treatment of loneliness of the aged.

Many older adults seem to have spent much of their own life denying their own needs and attending to the needs of others. While this has often been acknowledged as a liability by many, it can also be utilized as a potential asset. It must be remembered that a useful approach to handling social loneliness can be achieved by a movement toward other people while existential loneliness first requires a movement toward the self. With the older client, it is often easier to address *social* loneliness first since they often have a history of people-involvement as nurturers.

It appears that after the therapist has explored the lonely older adult's involvement with people as an approach to loneliness, it is often useful to use their interactions with others as "trigger points" for exploration of the self. Older people often find this difficult because they were raised in a less self-conscious culture and are not so familiar with their own internal needs as the contemporary therapist might assume. However, it appears universal that after the self has been discovered, there can be a less impeded approach to others. Therapists must be cautious here. Although the bulk of research equates healthy adjustment in old age to be highly correlated with level of social interaction, this does not necessarily disprove the earlier developmental theories of Jung (1933), Erikson (1959), or Cumming and Henry (1961) who equate satisfactory adjustment in old age with turning inward toward the self. It is quite possible that we are dealing with two types or levels of adjustment.

This leads to the necessary consideration of the paradoxical psychotherapeutic distinction between loneliness and solitude. Although loneliness is often experienced as a consequence of isolation it is not necessarily equated with the state of being alone. It also follows that one may feel lonely despite social interaction. According to Rubenstein and Shaver (1982), "solitude is a kind of positive aloneness. And, paradoxically, solitude can be a corrective for prolonged loneliness." This solitude produced a productive solution because of the relationship between active solitude and intimacy. The therapist *must* acknowledge that—as Rubenstein and Shaver argue— " in solitude we are intimate with ourselves in a way that enhances our intimacy with other people."

The therapist cannot ignore the fact that older adults are living in an increasingly secularized society where the traditional supports of the aged (such as religious organizations) are fast becoming less dominant in individual's lives. It falls to the therapist to provide clients with a format in treatment which enables them to achieve self-transcending concerns so that they may continue to be involved with people, as well as a developed sense of solitude and reflection so that they may assess the primordial issues of the meaning of life, death, atonement, and generativity.

The therapist will have to approach clients gingerly in the addressing of the issues of loneliness, solitude, and depression since direct insight into personal history (of a reconstructive nature) may be intolerable at this stage of life. It may be necessary to help the client sketch only the broadest outlines of personal history and make atonement on that basis. For example, in the chronically lonely client, it would be useful to sketch the broad history of the loneliness and to use this to assess the specific areas of behavioral deficit with some support and insight. The time is more usefully spent in focusing on corrective behaviors and enhanced social skills instead of uncovering, which may, depending on the physical conditions of the client, simply increase depression and anger with little positive impact for the already burdened client.

Finally, the client must acknowledge that people do not get old all at once. Attitudes, values, needs and expectations have developed over an extended life history. The therapist must strategize to frame these elements so that they can be appreciated, respected, and operationalized in such a mannner as to enable the individual to achieve at least modest and rewarding social interaction. In the recent film, *Cocoon*, the plight of many elderly is presented sensitively and in fantasy form. However, it is significant that in the film, although a number of individuals found a rejuvenating "fountain of youth," their energy resulted in increased behaviors which, in turn, energized them to further positively rewarding experiences. At the baseline of the film is the reality that those individuals who had refused risks for a lifetime always remained cautious, and *never* changed their behaviors—no matter what the potential reward. It remains the ongoing and sometimes indomitable challenge for the therapist to strategize interventions and modes of approach which will enable the aged client to, at least on a trial basis, explore and risk, then, finally, grow.

REFERENCES

Anderson, C. A., Horowitz, L. M., & French, R. (1983). Attritional style of lonely and depressed people. *Journal of Personality and Social Psychology*, *45*(1), 127-136.

Birren, J. E. & Renner, V. J. (1977). Research on the psychology of aging: Principles and experimentation. In J. E. Birren & K. W. Schaie, (Eds.) *Handbook of the psychology of aging*. New York: Van Nostrand.

Blum, J. E. & Tross S. (1980) Psychodynamic treatment of the elderly: A review of issues in theory and practice. In C. E. Eisedorfer (Ed.), *Annual review of gerontology & geriatrics Vol. 1*. New York: Springer Publishing Company.

Botwinick, J. (1978). *Aging and behavior: A comprehensive integration of research findings*, 2nd ed. New York: Springer Publishing Co.

Bousma, W. J. (1978). Christian adulthood. In E. H. Erikson (Ed.), *Adulthood*. New York: W. W. Norton & Co.

Brubaker, T. H., & Powers, E. A. (1976). The sterotype of the old. *Journal of Gerontology 31*, 441-447.

Busse, E. W., & Blazer, D. G. (1980). The theories and processes of aging. In *Handbook of geriatric psychiatry*. Van Nostrand New York: Reinhold Company.

Butler, R. (1969). Ageism: Another form of bigotry. *Gerontologist*, *9*, 243.

Cohen, G. D. (1980). Prospects for mental health and aging. In Birren & Sloane (Eds.), *Handbook of Mental Health and Aging*. New York: Van Nostrand.

Comfort, A. (1980). *Practice of geriatric psychiatry*. New York: Elsevier North Holland Inc.

Cumming, E. & Henry, W. E. (1961). *Growing old*. New York: Basic Books.

Dudley, C. J. & Hillery, G. A. (1977). Freedom and alienation in homes for the aged. *Gerontolgist*, *17*(2), 140.

Epstein, G., Weitz, L., Roback, H., & McKee. (1975). Research on Bereavement: A selective critical review. *Comprehensive Psychiatry*, *16*, 537-546.

Erikson, E. H. (1959). *Identity and the life cycle. Psychological Issues Monograph I*. New York: International University Press.

George, L. K. (1980). *Role transitions in later life*. Monterey, CA: Brooks/Cole Publishing Co.

Gutmann, D. (1978). Life events and decision making by older adults. *Gerontologist*, *18*(5 part 1), 462-467.

Gutmann, D. (1980). Observations on culture and mental health in later life. Birren & Sloane (Eds.) *Handbook of mental health and aging*. Englewood Cliffs, NJ: Prentice-Hall.

Hareven, T. (1978). The last stage: Historical adulthood and old age. In E. H. Erikson (Ed.), *Adulthood*. New York: W. W. Norton & Co.

Harris, L. & Associates (1975). *The myth and reality of aging in america*. Washington, DC: The National Council on Aging.

Hendricks, J., & Hendricks, C. D. (1977). *Aging in a mass society: Myths and realities*. Cambridge, MA: Winthrop.

Hunter, K. I., & Linn, M. W. (1980-81). Psychosocial differences between elderly volunteers and non-volunteers. *International Journal of Aging & Human Development*, *12*(3), 205-213.

Ingram, D. K., & Barry, J. R. (1977). National statistics on deaths in nursing homes: Interpretations and implications. *Gerontologist*, *17*, 303-308.

Jung, C. G. (1933). *Modern man in search of a soul*. New York: Harcourt Brace Jovanovich.

Kalish, R. The religious triad: Church, clergy and faith in the resources network. *Generations*, *3*, 27.

Keefer, C. (1980). Loneliness and Japanese social structure: In Hartog, Audy, & Cohen (Eds.), *The anatomy of loneliness*. New York: International Universities Press.

Landau, J. (1980). Loneliness and creativity. In Hartog, Audy, & Cohen (Eds.), *The anatomy of loneliness*. New York: International Universities Press.

Larson, R. (1978). Thirty years of research on the subjective well-being of older Americans. *Journal of Gerontology*, *33*, 109-29.

Lazarus, L. W. (1980). Selfpsychology and psychotherapy with the elderly: Theory and practice. *Journal of Geriatric Psychiatry*, *13*(1), 69-88.

Lopata, H. Z. (1980). Loneliness in widowhood. In Hartog, Audy, & Cohen (Eds.), *The Anatomy of loneliness*. New York: International Universities Press.

Mancini, J. A. (1980-1981). Effects of health and income on control orientation and life satisfaction among aged public residents. *International Journal of Aging and Human Development*, *12*(3), 215-220.

McClelland, K. (1980). Self-conception and Life satisfaction: Integrating aged subculture and activity theory. *Journal of Gerontology*, *37*(6), 723-732.

Owens, C. M. (1981). Meditation as a solution to the problem of aging. In R. Kastenbaum (Ed.), *Old age on the new scene*. New York: Springer Publishing Co.

Palmore, E. (1980). The social factors in aging. In E. W. Busse & D. G. Blazer (Eds.), *Handbook of geriatric psychiatry*. New York: Van Nostrand Reinhold Co.

Payne, E. C. (1975). Depression and suicide. In J. G. Howell (Ed.), *Modern perspectives in psychiatry of old age*. New York: Brunner/Mazel.

Peterson, J. A. (1980). Social-psychological aspects of death and dying and mental health. In Birren & Sloane (Eds.), *Handbook of mental health and aging*. Englewood Cliffs, NJ: Prentice-Hall.

Reid, D. W., Haas, G., & Harkings, D. (1977). Locus of desired control and positive self-concepts of the elderly. *Journal of Gerontology*, *32*(4).

Rubenstein, C. & Shaver, P. (1982). *In search of intimacy*. New York: Delacorte Press.

Snow, R. & Crapo, L. (1982). Emotional bondedness, subjective well-being and health in elderly medical patients. *Journal of Gerontology*, *37*(5), 609-615.

Staser, C. W. & Staser, H. T. (1976). Organized religion: Community considerations. In H. J. Oyer & J. Oyer (Eds.), *Aging and communication*. Baltimore: University Park Press.

Statistical abstract of the United States 1982-83, 103rd Ed.

Steur, J. (1982). Psychotherapy for depressed elders. In D. G. Blazer (Ed.), *Depression in late life*. St. Louis: C. V. Mosby Co.

Tillich, P. (1980). Loneliness and solitude. In Hartog, Audy, & Cohen (Eds.), *The anatomy of loneliness*. New York: International Universities Press.

Wigdor, B. T. (1980). Drives and motivations with aging. In Birren & Sloane (Eds.), *Handbook of mental health and aging*. Englewood Cliffs, NJ: Prentice-Hall.

Yurich, A. G., Robb, S. S., Spier, B. E., & Ebert, N. J. (1980). *The aged person and the nursing process*. New York: Appleton-Century-Crofts.

Replication of the Phenomenology of Loneliness in the Therapeutic Dyad

Douglas L. Gerardi

ABSTRACT. This paper will illustrate a possible countertransference phenomenon. Through a brief theoretical discussion, supplemented by clinical vignettes, the following position will be developed: The therapist may contribute to the patient's experience of loneliness when he or she intervenes without a recognition of self as a contributor to the interactive process.

THE THERAPEUTIC SETTING: THE THERAPIST COMMUNICATES WITH THE PATIENT

A model of psychotherapy which suggests an interactive process occurring between patient and therapist requires adoption of several assumptions:

1. It is necessary to clearly, comprehensively, and consistently describe the ongoing input of the therapist as a stimulus to which the patient responds.
2. It is necessary to establish a standard for this stimulus. Such establishment of and conscientious adherence to the standard will allow for a clear analysis of the therapist's contribution to the process, as distinct from the patient's contribution.
3. The patient's activity in the interactive process can be understood as a unique, idiosyncratic response to the stimulus of the therapist's input, and will reflect the emotional core or personality of the patient.

Various attempts to prescribe the most appropriate style of therapist activity have been evident in the literature. Freud presented guidelines for

Dr. Gerardi maintains a private practice in Philadelphia, PA. He is a faculty member of the Lenox Hill Hospital Psychotherapy Program at Lenox Hill Hospital, Manhattan, New York. Mail requests for reprints to Dr. Douglas L. Gerardi, 1134 Rodman Street, House #3, Philadelphia, PA 19147.

the therapist to adhere to in psychoanalytic treatment through his technique papers (see Freud 1961/1900, 1912, 1913, 1914, 1915).* Other writers (Greenson 1967; Langs 1982, 1985a, 1985b; Stone 1961) have contributed to a fuller understanding and elaboration of the behaviors a therapist should follow to provide sound and relatively countertransference-free input.[1]

Following from the above-stated assumptions regarding the therapist's communication to the patient, corollaries of the patient's communication to the therapist can be posited. Each of these corollaries rests on the adoption of the assumptions regarding the therapeutic setting, as operationalized through the therapist's interventions.[2]

Patient corollaries to the assumptions regarding the therapist's input are:

1. An explanation of all patient behaviors as responses to the stimuli generated by the therapist (i.e., interventions) is appropriate, valid, and interpretable if the therapist input is constantly and conscientiously monitored.
2. As the therapist adheres to a standard of interventions, it is possible to clearly specify the patient behaviors which are distortions (i.e., transference) and represent manifestations of psychopathology. As the therapist deviates from the established standard, it is impossible to accurately assign patient behaviors to the category of distortion (i.e., transference) or a category of responses to unconscious perceptions of the therapist (i.e., non-transference).
3. The patient's behavior, given countertransference-free input from the therapist, will contain the key emotional disturbances which manifest themselves in symptomatic form.

If the therapist contaminates the bipersonal field (Langs 1976) with

---

*Although these papers pertain to psychoanalysis, they are cited as relevant because the principles described in this paper apply to both psychoanalysis and psychotherapy.

[1]Many diverse views of "countertransference" have been offered in the literature. For the purposes of this paper, the following definition is suggested: Countertransference is the whole gamut of therapist behaviors (i.e., thoughts, words, feelings, overt actions) which stem from the therapist's own unresolved issues and which may or may not be monitored and checked by the therapist. Should the therapist intervene on behalf of his countertransference, he will tend to elicit from the patient unconscious negative and essentially harmful perceptions of himself.

[2]For the purposes of this paper, the following definition of intervention is adopted:
The interventions of the therapist include all aspects of his or her establishment of the setting, development and management of the ground rules of therapy; silences and verbal interventions of all types; the therapist's self-revelations, including personal information obtained by the patient about the therapist from other sources; the therapist's active or implicit sanction of third party involvement in the treatment; the prescription of medication; and anything else pertaining to or done by the therapist that has bearing on the psychotherapeutic experience. (Langs, 1985a, p. 4)

countertransference-based interventions, the patient will be distracted from his or her expression of symptoms and instead will respond to the therapist's errors in technique. Searles (1975) has suggested that the patient unconsciously attempts to cure the therapist in the presence of countertransference.

Building upon earlier writings (Freud 1900), specifically the notion of derivative expression in the patient's associations, Langs (1985a) suggests the patients' material be monitored for its latent meanings. Derivative communication, characterized by displacement and symbolization, is seen as the mode by which the patient unconsciously comments on the spiraling interactive process between the therapist and himself or herself. Through derivative communication, the patient will unconsciously "supervise" the therapist, and through the use of displacement and symbolization will portray the therapist's technical errors.

THE THERAPIST'S CONTRIBUTION TO THE PATIENT'S PHENOMENOLOGY OF LONELINESS

Classical Freudian theories of loneliness have focused on the vicissitudes of childhood as causal in the adult's experience of loneliness. Specifically, the phenomenology of loneliness can be seen as an affective symptom which represents a compromise formation. The compromise is between the expression of an instinctual drive emanating from the id, which is opposed by the prohibitive forces of the superego (Brenner 1982). The resultant experience of loneliness ensues as the ego carries out its adaptive function for the organism. Contemporary psychoanalytic theorists writing from an object-relations perspective tend to view emotional disturbance as arising from the ego's frustrated attempts at object-seeking. Fairburn (1952) has stated that the ego is object-seeking from birth. Both classical and contemporary approaches have tended to stress the past experience of the individual, attributing affect experienced in the therapeutic relationship to transference. This paper will explore the concept of the patient's unconscious perception of the therapist's activity as communicated through the patient's derivatives. As such, the focus will be on the "here and now" determinants, as opposed to transference, which replicate the experience of loneliness in the therapeutic relationship.

Langs (1979, 1982) has suggested the framework of the therapeutic environment which best facilitates the expression of unconscious conflict, and provides the optimum holding environment for the client. His "communicative" approach to psychotherapy stresses the importance of understanding appropriate management of the "frame" of the psychotherapy. Chief among the characteristics of the secure frame are the following: set time and meeting place, absence of third parties to the treatment, appropriate and consistent fee, appropriate physical setting, relative anonymity, total privacy and confidentiality, and therapist neutrality. The therapist interprets the patient's derivative communication within the secure frame. When the frame has not been secured or is disrupted, the patient's derivatives will convey unconscious encoded perceptions of the therapist, rather than transference fantasies. Drawing upon Freud's (1900) writings on dreams, and influenced by the Kleinian school as represented by Bion (1977), Langs defines derivative communication as the language medium or working vocabulary of the unconscious. Langs has coined the term "adaptive context" to define that part of the ongoing interactive process of therapy which the therapist contributes. The adaptive context stimulates a perception of the therapist. This perception is a result of a here-and-now aspect of the therapist's activity. This activity falls into two main categories: (1) interventions and interpretations offered by the therapist, (2) therapist's management of the framework of the psychotherapy. Those adaptive contexts which tend to replicate the experience of loneliness in the therapeutic dyad, will be illustrated through clinical vignettes from two consecutive therapy sessions. Specific attention will be focused on frame issues.

Clinical Illustration

The patient, Mr. A., is a 32-year-old male who recently completed law school. He had one previous treatment experience in a clinic setting. He sought therapy at that time because of his periods of depression and anxiety, as well as relationship problems with his fiancée. In the clinic setting, he was seen initially in individual therapy. After a few months of treatment his therapist recommended couples therapy, whereupon he and his fiancée were seen together for several months. The patient reported that this first treatment experience was helpful, although he was confused about the shift from individual to couples therapy, and back to individual therapy. The treatment ended rather abruptly, as the patient's insurance-policy clauses for psychotherapy stipulated a fixed number of sessions per year. The patient then requested a referral from his therapist and was given the name of a private practitioner.

Mr. A. is one of three siblings. He is the youngest child with two older sisters. He describes a rather conflicted relationship with both parents. He recalls several poignant interactions with his mother which appear to have left him with a highly ambivalent sense of emotional bonding to her. He reports that when he was a child, his mother would provide graphic details of the difficult labor she endured prior to his delivery. He recalls that these interactions with his mother occurred after he had committed some minor "offense," usually some harmless action such as lateness for dinner or failure to complete household chores. He recalls his mother as being subtly critical of his performance in academics as well as in athletics. This subtle disapproval took the form of emotional withdrawal wherein his mother would not speak to him for a few days except for the necessary interactions. He recalls trying to figure out, as a child, what infraction he had committed to cause his mother to withdraw her attention from him.

He describes his father as a "closet alcholic" who would occasionally come home after a drunken binge and beat his mother and sister. At those times, he fled from his father, usually running to a neighbor's house to escape the physical altercation. He recalled, as a child, being confused about his father's actions and inconsistency. He spent some time in the therapy describing sustained periods of intense loneliness. He recalled one particularly poignant childhood scene. He was an avid model-builder throughout childhood and adolescence. He had spent considerable time building a sophisticated motorized model of a World War II destroyer, intending to enter it in a competition. The contest was billed as a father-and-son event. He recalled working on the model with his father. His father was a skilled craftsman by training and occupation. He remembered wanting to work more cooperatively on the project with his father, but instead he reported that his father monopolized the work, often ignoring his son's attempts to work on the model. The day of the competition arrived. Father and son registered, whereupon the father went off to a refreshment stand, stating he would return shortly in time for the competition. The afternoon wore on, with son waiting for father to return. He did not appear for the scheduled event, but rather, spent the afternoon drinking beer, forgetting about his son. When he did return, he was staggering drunk and the son had to call up his mother to come drive both him and his drunken father home.

This material is offered to illustrate how this particular patient would be exquisitely sensitive to framework issues in the therapy relationship, given his dynamics and genetics. The framework of the therapy relationship symbolically represents the frame or hold of the psychological environment provided by the parent for the child.

The two consecutive sessions, condensed for illustration here, immediately followed an extended break in the treatment, due to the therapist's vacation. Although announced at the onset of the treatment as a month-long break, this adaptive context imposed by the therapist is particularly relevant in that the break was extended to 5 weeks. During the last session before the break, the therapist announced that she would be away for an additional week. The sessions presented occurred approximately one year into the individual treatment. The frame has been consistently and progressively secured, as the patient's derivatives permitted interpretation and rectification.

Session I

(The patient arrives 15 minutes late for a 45-minute session.)

The patient begins with a "welcome back from your vacation" statement to the therapist, then lapses into a silence of several minutes. He then goes on to recall that last session he spoke about returning from a vacation of a few days in North Carolina. He went on to recall that he had missed a session in early July. He remembered talking about breaking up with Sue, a girlfriend of almost one year. He went on to talk about leaving her in the park after they had a heated discussion. He left her alone in the park after the interaction. He stated he was reluctant to leave her alone. He went on to state he hadn't seen her for almost 3 or 4 weeks now. He ran into her on the street outside his office during a lunch break. He was surprised to find her happy and smiling. He wondered why she wasn't as miserable as he had been because of their breakup. He decided to call her that evening. He told her during that conversation that he had been miserable and she confided to him that she too was miserable. He suggested they get together for dinner the next evening, and Sue agreed. The dinner date quite coincidentally fell within one week of the first anniversary of their first date. They went out to dinner and then returned to Sue's apartment. He was confused as to whether she wanted him to spend the night.

It got to be about 2 o'clock in the morning. While Sue was in the bathroom, he undressed and hopped into bed. When Sue stepped into the bedroom, she said "What a turkey!". He told her she better call the police. Sue told him to put his clothes back on. He got dressed and started to walk out of the bedroom when Sue said, "Hey wait a minute, I didn't mean get dressed right now, I meant tomorrow morning." Sue then jumped into bed and Mr. A. spent the night. He said the sex was wonderful. He reported that Sue was confusing to him; She seemed ambivalent about how she was going to relate to him and what she wanted from him. He wished she would be clear and consistent.

(Silence of several minutes.)

Mr. A. then went on to say that he had been very depressed for the past few weeks. He felt he was dealing well with the depression, and that exercise seemed to help a great deal with it. He reported that he had been dating a number of women. He started to date a paralegal in his office. She seemed to have many interests; archaeology, music, astronomy, sailing. He was beginning to feel that it's important to be selective because the stakes are high when you're in a relationship. Mr. A. then said that a few years ago he would quickly rush into relationships, quickly becoming infatuated with a woman. Now he knows he has to take things slower. He went on to talk about Marsha, a psychiatrist whom he had dated a couple of times. He feels she's very nice. She seems to listen attentively when he talks. She seems to be interested in him. He would like her to talk more though.

(Silence of several minutes, during which Mr. A. feels a blister on his hand. He appears to be unaware of this activity, almost distracted as he stares ahead for several minutes.)

He goes on to say he's spent his whole life trying to live up to others' expectations of him. People have always thought he was a bit strange. They never appreciated his dry sense of humor.

(Several minutes of silence.)

Mr. A. goes on to report that he had a client in his office the previous morning and was taking information to prepare a case. His mind was wandering as the client was speaking, and the client asked him if he understood what he just said. Mr. A. had been so far into his thoughts about Sue that he hadn't heard what the client was talking about. He had to ask the client to repeat himself. He reported that he felt foolish and irresponsible. He then went on to say that he was glad the therapist was back. He was looking forward to a year of growth in therapy.

(The therapist was suffering from allergies and was sniffling throughout the session.)

Mr. A. commented that it sounded like the therapist had a cold. He suggested she take vitamin C. He concluded the session by remarking he was glad the therapist was back.

Session I: Analysis and Discussion

It's significant to note that the patient draws attention to the frame of the therapy by appearing 15 minutes late for the session. It can be interpreted that this communication was an unconscious attempt to alert the therapist to an impairment in the relationship. Technically speaking, this "indicator" (Langs, 1985) is a gross behavioral resistance. In addition, the several minutes' silence at the beginning of the session is a reenactment of the lapse in the therapy due to the therapist's absence. The patient next recalls that in the last session he spoke about his own vacation of a few days in North Carolina. In terms of derivative communication the patient may be using displacement. He is manifestly mentioning his own vacation, but he may be unconsciously representing the therapist's vacation. The patient next recalls that he had missed a session in early July. Again, the patient may be derivatively referring to the missed session brought about by the therapist's extension of her vacation by an additional week. The patient goes on to bring up the topic of breaking up with his girlfriend, Sue. He brings up an image of leaving her in the park alone. This theme of aloneness is highlighted by the patient's adding that he hasn't seen Sue in almost 3 or 4 weeks now. The patient may be derivatively communicating his experience of the break in the treatment. More specifically, the image of someone being left alone may be a portrayal of the patient's phenomenology of the break in the treatment. The patient then goes on to describe running into Sue on the street and reported feeling surprised that Sue appeared happy, while he was miserable. This may be interpreted as an unconscious perception of the therapist's phenomenology of the break in the therapy, again conveyed in derivative form utilizing the mechanism of displacement. This may also relate to the dynamic and genetic underpinnings of Mr. A.'s history of depression. Specifically, separations may be experienced as abandonments, wherein he experiences distress while the abandoner appears unaffected. (The reader is reminded of the background history previously reported here, specifically Mr. A.'s childhood interactions with his parents.)

The next segment of material, Mr. A's dinner date with Sue, is characterized by themes of confusion in communication and interpersonal relationships, a compromise in relationship boundaries, and ambivalence and unclarity regarding participation in a relationship. These themes can be interpreted as a manifestation of the patient's unconscious commentary on the current status of the therapy relationship, as well as an unconscious perception of a therapist who has failed to keep the frame of the therapy secure. The emergence of instinctual material of a sexual nature is significant here. As the therapist fails to maintain the security of the frame, the patient may tend to produce derivatives laden with instinctual drive themes, conveying the patient's unconscious perceptions of the therapist (Langs, 1985, personal communication).

Next, several minutes of silence ensued in the session. At this point, the therapist had sufficient material to offer an intervention, but failed to do so. In supervision following the session, the therapist reported feeling somewhat awkward and "communicatively deaf" during the session. Having been away from the therapy for a total of 5 weeks gave her a feeling of staleness. It is also significant to note that this therapist had been studying the communicative approach and was trying to continually monitor the material along communicative guidelines. Most relevantly, the therapist reported feeling guilty about the extended break in the treatment, particularly the extended period of the additional week. The therapist appreciated the influence the adaptive context of the break would have on the therapy, but was unable to offer an appropriate intervention. From a technical point of view, the patient had supplied the necessary ingredients for an intervention. Specifically, the patient had mentioned the adaptive context of the therapist's break, a rich derivative complex which coalesced around the mentioned adaptive context and revealed the resonance of the adaptive context with the patient's unconscious, the patient's unconscious perception of the therapist, and finally the patient's reactions to perceptions of the therapist.

At this point, a new adaptive context has been introduced into the therapy, namely a missed intervention. The session will now have to be monitored for two adaptive contexts: (1) the therapist's vacation with abruptly announced extension (2) the missed intervention.

After the prolonged silence, itself an indicator of a disruption in the optimal holding environment of the therapy relationship, Mr. A. reports he's been very depressed for the past few weeks. His comment that "exercise seemed to help a great deal" with the depression may be interpreted as a derivative comment conveying the patient's frustration with therapy and his consequent sense of hopelessness that therapy will help him resolve his depression. Thus he must seek an alternative means of coping with depression, namely exercise. The next segment of material, wherein Mr. A. reports on the two new relationships he has begun, is prefaced by Mr. A.'s comment that he feels the need to be selective in relationships and take things slower. He may be conveying how the missed intervention has affected him. His narrative regarding Marsha, the psychiatrist, is a poignant derivative perception of the therapist who has missed an intervention, and conveys a "model of rectification" (Langs 1982) for the therapist. The patient is commenting on the therapist's technique, through displacement, and is requesting that the therapist offer an intervention. The ensuing silence and Mr. A.'s behavior of rubbing the blister on his hand poignantly conveys the patient's sense of loneliness and his attempt to provide self-stimulation and soothing attention in the presence of an inattentive, and specifically for Mr. A., an abandoning therapist. He next goes on to reveal a dynamic which explains his symptom of depression. Specifically, a pattern of attempts to live up to others' expectations and ultimately not winning the much-sought-after approval because people always thought he was a bit strange. A possible explanation for the emergence of this material at this point in the session is the following: The patient has introjected the therapist's technical error of the missed intervention and has turned it into a self-recrimination.

The patient continues with another indicator of silence and then offers an unconscious perception of the therapist who has missed an intervention. Again utilizing derivative communication and displacement, the patient produces an image of a professional who is impaired in his professional duties. Although producing a narrative of himself being distracted in his thoughts and irresponsible in his obligations to his client, he may be derivatively conveying his perception of the therapist's missed intervention and his unconscious assumptions regarding the reasons for the therapist's missed intervention. Specifically, he assumes the therapist has missed the intervention because she was preoccupied with her own problems. The patient concludes the session by recommending a treatment to the therapist for her cold. In this regard, an interesting role reversal has taken place. The designated patient becomes the functional therapist, and the designated therapist assumes the role of functional patient. This role reversal can be interpreted as the result of the therapist's failure to intervene which leads to the patient's unconscious perception of the therapist as one who needs treatment.

Session II

(The patient arrives on time for the session.)

The patient begins the session by inquiring how the therapist's cold is and adds he was concerned about the therapist last session. He adds that he hopes she's feeling better. He comments that her cold was probably due to the stress of the therapist ending her vacation.

(Silence of several minutes)

Mr. A. goes on to report that he's been symptomatic this past week; actually, he felt that his symptoms peaked this past week. However, he added that he's felt bad for about 3 weeks. He reported that he had been depressed and anxious. He said that he made the decision to stop taking sleeping pills that he started about 3 weeks ago. He decided to start taking medication to help him sleep because the depression and anxiety were the worst he had ever experienced. Despite this though, he decided that he wouldn't take sleep medication last night. As a result he reports he had horrible nightmares all night long, one after the other. All he could remember was that he was being chased. He looked in a mirror and saw himself and he looked horrible, like he needed sleep. He said that he was trying to keep himself in the swing of things. He said that he was keeping up with his work in the office, but only because the workload was down, and that if things were more busy he really wouldn't be able to keep up with the job responsibilities. He saw a lot of sickness around him. Sickness and death. It seemed he knew a lot of people who were dealing with illness and death. It's very depressing. He said his partner in the law practice was dealing with his mother's illness. She's dying of cancer. His partner told him that he was sure his mother and father thought they had many more years together, and now one of them will be left alone. Another friend of his also has a parent dying of cancer. Maybe it has gotten to him, he said. He's probably really run down and physically ill. He said he knows he's got emotional problems.

(Silence of several minutes)

He reports he was disappointed last night with his dinner with Pam. She's the new woman he's been seeing. He had a lot of expectations and hope for that relationship. Last night he and Pam talked about their feeling of incompatibility. He was thinking he needs to keep plugging away and just keep his options open. He added that "you never can tell with relationships . . . how they'll turn out." If things go sour that quickly with someone he was that excited about, well, then he guesses he just didn't know . . . He felt he shouldn't get so excited so quickly. Sue and he met and they spent the night together last night. He knew that probably would confuse things between them, but he said he just didn't want to be alone. He was afraid of being alone.

(Silence of several minutes)
(The therapist next offers an intervention)

> T: You began the session this evening by mentioning my vacation. You then went on to report you've been anxious and depressed. You began to medicate yourself, but decided to stop. Tonight you bring up images of relationships ending, relationships being frustrated, and impaired, and relationships ending in death, and your fear of being left alone. You were so frightened about being alone that you spent the night with Sue. You may be telling me that in some way, my vacation has led to your feeling depressed and anxious and you thus perceived me as not living up to my responsibilities as a therapist. You may have felt that in the therapy here, I've impaired our relationship. You experienced me as leaving the therapy and you thus began an alternative treatment by medicating yourself.

(Silence of several minutes.)
Mr. A. responded he didn't think this had to do so much with the therapist's vacation. After all, he added, he felt the therapist was entitled to a break from her job. He added he was feeling depressed and alone about his breakup with Sue. Sometimes he felt like he needed a break from looking at himself so intensely. He said he felt the vacation was a vacation from looking at himself so intensely. He decided to take his own vacation while the therapist was away. He added everyone needs to get away once in awhile.
(Silence of several minutes.)
He said that as he heard himself talking, it gave him a chance to just sit back and look at how depressed he felt. He keeps plugging away though. He thinks that's always been one of his strong points. He doesn't give up. He's a fighter.
(Silence of a few minutes till end of session)

Session II: Analysis and Discussion

The reader is reminded that two adaptive contexts are now active at the start of this session: (1) the therapist's vacation with the abruptly announced extension (2) the missed intervention of Session I. The therapist will need to listen during this session for derivatives which coalesce around these two adaptive contexts and convey both the unconscious resonance of these adaptive contexts with the patient's unconscious, as well as the patient's unconscious perception of the therapist in light of these two adaptive contexts. In addition, the patient's reaction to these perceptions, in light of the adaptive contexts, should be monitored. As the security of the frame has now been impaired, the patient will respond to the impairment as his primary adaptive task. His material will be seen as reflecting perceptions of the therapist, as opposed to revealing transference manifestations.

The session begins with the patient arriving on time. This behavior is contrasted with the 15-minute lateness with which the patient began the previous session. This can be interpreted as the patient presenting the therapist with a model of sound functioning, regarding the security of the frame. Adherence to timeliness by the patient is also seen as an unconscious communication to the therapist, highlighting the need for timely interventions. It's important to note that the patient appears to continue the role reversal initiated at the end of the previous session, by inquiring about the therapist's cold and thus assuming the role, symbolically, of the functional therapist. By inquiring about the therapist's cold, the patient is remotely alluding to the previous session, thus drawing the therapist's awareness to that session and alerting her that something is unresolved about it. It is also significant to note that the patient again manifestly represents the adaptive context of the therapist's vacation. Such manifest representations of an adaptive context so early in a session is a sign that the rest of the session will serve as an arena for the patient to derivatively portray the unique, idiosyncratic, unconscious meanings of the adaptive context for him, as well as perceptions of the therapist and reactions to these perceptions.

The patient next provides an indicator in the form of silence. He goes on to report his depression and anxiety which have peaked since the last session. He added he's been experiencing these symptoms for 3 weeks or so. Here it can be seen that although Mr. A. does not manifestly mention the therapist's vacation, the time frame of his reported symptoms corresponds to the break in therapy. He goes on to report that the depression and anxiety were the worst he ever experienced, prompting him to take medication to help him sleep. When he stopped the sleeping pills, horrible nightmares ensued, and he "looked horrible" in the dream. He reports keeping up in his work, but only because the workload has been light. He then brings up images of sickness and death and ultimately, the image of someone being left "all alone."

The first segment of this session can be seen as reflecting an increase in the patient's symptoms. The image of a professional barely keeping up with his work can be seen as an unconscious perception of the therapist who has not kept up with her responsibilities by providing an appropriate intervention. The images of sickness and death and someone left "all alone" can be seen as a poignant portrayal of the replication of the phenomenology of loneliness in the therapy relationship.

After several minutes of silence, Mr. A. goes on to report his disappointment in a relationship with Pam. The notion of incompatibility was discussed. He goes on to talk about the unpredictability of relationships.

He needs to keep his options open. He brings up the theme of "being alone" again. Despite the feeling that sleeping with Sue would confuse, his fear of being alone overcame him. These derivatives all coalesce nicely around the adaptive context of the missed intervention. The theme of "being alone" is continued.

The therapist's intervention was a good attempt at dealing with the adaptive context of the therapist's vacation and the consequent break in therapy, however the technical error appears to lie in the timing of the intervention. This intervention would have been timely had it been delivered in the last session. The derivatives in this session appear to coalesce more precisely around the adaptive context of the missed intervention from the last session. It's significant to note that the patient began this session by remotely referring to the last session via his inquiry about the therapist's cold. This should have sensitized the therapist to hear the ensuing session in light of the missed intervention.

The patient responds to the intervention with prolonged silence. He then manifestly rejects the intervention, and appears to manifestly approve of the vacation. A prolonged silence follows. The ensuing material contains an image of a person sitting back and listening to himself, and in so doing, achieving some self-knowledge. This can be interpreted as the patient's unconscious reaction to the intervention and his "supervision" of the therapist. Namely, the therapist should listen carefully to what she says and in so doing achieve some insight into her functioning as a therapist. The patient proceeds with a positive image of a person persevering and plugging away. He seems to be saying that he unconsciously perceives the therapist as trying to help, even though she has not intervened as accurately or appropriately as she might have. He appreciates her plugging away and sticking with the task.

It's suggested that a "playback" (Langs 1985) of selected derivatives would have been an appropriate intervention. As the patient did not mention the missed intervention, it would be premature to offer an intervention involving this adaptive context. Rather, a playing back of all the derivatives which coalesced around the missed intervention would be indicated. Such a playback would facilitate the patient's naming of the adaptive context, and would thus pave the way for a fuller interpretation. This interpretation would optimally reveal to the patient how the adaptive context elicited selected unconscious perceptions of the therapist and consequently how the patient reacted symptomatically to these perceptions.

As therapists become sensitive to the unconscious implications of their interventions, particularly frame management, they will provide a sound psychological environment within which patients can communciate effectively. Establishing such an environment will be the best insurance against therapists' repeating traumatic behaviors which ultimately result in the experience of loneliness for the patient.

REFERENCES

Bion, W. (1977). *Seven servants.* New York: Jason Aronson.

Brenner, C. (1982). *The mind in conflict.* New York: International Universities Press.

Fairbairn, W.R.D. (1952). *An object relations theory of the personality.* London, New York: Basic Books.

Freud, S. (1961). The interpretation of dreams. In J. Strachey (Ed. and Trans.), *The standard edition of the complete psychological works of Sigmund Freud* (Vols. 4 & 5). London: Hogarth Press. (Original work published 1900).

Freud, S. (1961). The dynamics of transference. In J. Strachey (Ed. and Trans.). *The standard edition of the complete psychological works of Sigmund Freud* (Vol 12, pp. 97-108). London: Hogarth. (Original work published 1912).

Freud, S. (1961). Observations on transference love. In J. Strachey (Ed. and Trans.), *The standard edition of the complete psychological works of Sigmund Freud* (Vol. 12, pp. 157-171). London: Hogarth Press. (Original work published 1915).

Freud, S. (1961). On beginning the treatment. In J. Strachey (Ed. and Trans.), *The standard edition of the complete psychological works of Sigmund Freud* (Vol. 12, pp. 121-144). London: Hogarth Press. (Original work published 1913).

Freud, S. (1961). Recommendations to physicians practising psycho-analysis. In J. Strachey (Ed. and Trans.), *The standard edition of the complete psychological works of Sigmund Freud* (Vol. 12, pp. 111-120). London: Hogarth Press. (Original work published 1912).

Freud, S. (1961). Remembering, repeating and working through. In J. Strachey (Ed. and Trans.), *The complete psychological works of Sigmund Freud* (Vol. 12, pp. 145-156). London: Hogarth Press. (Original work published 1914).

Greenson, R. (1967). *The technique and practice of psychoanalysis.* New York: International Universities Press.

Langs, R. (1976). *The Bipersonal field.* New York: Jason Aronson.

Langs, R. (1979). *The therapeutic environment.* New York: Jason Aronson.

Langs, R. (1982). *Psychotherapy: A basic text.* New York: Jason Aronson.

Langs, R. (1985a). *Workbooks for psychotherapists. Vol. II: Listening and formulating.* Emerson, NJ: Newconcept Press.

Langs, R. (1985b). *Workbooks for psychotherapist. Vol. III: Intervening and validating.* Emerson, NJ: Newconcept Press.

Searles, H. (1975). The patient as therapist to his analyst. In P. Giovacchini (Ed.), *Tactics and techniques in psychoanalytic therapy* (pp. 95-151). New York: Jason Aronson.

Stone, L. (1961). *The psychoanaltyic situation.* New York: International Universities Press.

Winnicott, D.W. (1965). *The maturational process and the facilitating environment.* New York: International Universities Press.

A Model for Working
With Lonely Clients:
Sadler Revisited

Lee J. Richmond
Edith D. Picken

ABSTRACT. This article offers direction for people who counsel growing numbers of lonely clients by connecting Sadler's cosmic cultural,
social, interpersonal and psychological loneliness to both causes and consequences. Treatment that involves awareness, identification, personalization and entry into positive solitude is suggested. Illustrative case studies
are included.

Loneliness, the subjective experience of being isolated from one's environment, has been recognized since the 1970s as a psychological problem of frightening proportions (Sadler, 1974; Satran, 1975; Weiss,
1973). Defined as a feeling of isolated selfhood (Sobosan, 1978) and an
experience of being alone, solitary, and cut off from others (Webster's
New World Dictionary, 1978), Fromm-Reichmann (1959) described
loneliness as ''such a painful, frightening experience that people do prac-
tically everything to avoid it.'' Few argue that its effects can be corrosive
of self-esteem, leading to a downward spiraling that for some people includes serious damage along with discomfort. Despite the potential se-
riousness of the consequences of loneliness, the phenomenon is little
researched and comparatively little discussed in psychological literature.
Various explanations have been offered. One explanation is that loneliness is difficult to isolate from other variables such as separation anxiety,
fear, guilt, and depression. Another is that loneliness, like death, is an uncomfortable subject and one with which psychologists, like other people,
become exceedingly uncomfortable. A more probable explanation, advanced by Sadler (1978), is that loneliness is a subjective experience
rather than an easily identifiable behavior or event. Furthermore, it is an
experience with a reflexive component. To be lonely, one must perceive

Lee J. Richmond, Ph.D., is Professor of Counseling and Human Development, The John
Hopkins University, and Psychologist in private practice, Baltimore, Md. Edith D. Picken is Gradu-
ate Student in Counseling and Human Development at John Hopkins University and High School
Counselor, Chesapeake High School, Anne Arundel Co., Md.

oneself as separate from others. Therefore, to fully examine this phenomenon, a phenomenological approach rather than a behavioral approach must be taken. Self-report data rather than experimental data are valued. This methodology has been considered "unscientific" by most academic psychologists.

Psychoanalysts, on the other hand, have considered the topic important. Harry Stack Sullivan (1953) thought loneliness could be a more powerful force than anxiety in shaping individual behavior. To him, loneliness was a potent force with enough driving power to force some individuals to overcome anxiety and achieve companionship. Sullivan was not alone. At the time of her death, after many years of studying the subject, Fromm-Reichmann (1959) left an unfinished paper on the subject of loneliness. In this paper she lamented the fact that loneliness was poorly conceptualized. She complained that in one basket were lumped "aloneness, isolation, loneliness in cultural groups, self-imposed loneliness, compulsory solitude, and real loneliness."

Englehart (1974), Moustakas (1961), and Sadler (1974, 1978), call for a needed distinction between loneliness and solitude. Although both are identified by reflexive self-referent characteristics, the latter, often sought by mystics, artists, poets, and persons seeking self-renewal is generally seen to provide positive benefit. A sense of presence, personal or universal, rather than loss, is often the product of solitude.

Nor is loneliness isolation. One can be physically or socially isolated without experiencing the subjective feeling of loneliness, and one can experience loneliness in a crowd. Similarly, alienation does not imply loneliness per se. Nevertheless, as Sadler (1978) points out, *Psychological Abstracts* does not carry a listing under the heading of loneliness, but instead refers readers to other headings such as alienation or isolation, though each may be quite different from the phenomenon in question.

For counselors and therapists all of this provides a serious dilemma. Because there is no congruent theory of loneliness there is little research on the subject. Because there is little research there is little direction for clinicians about how best to assess and treat lonely people. There are, however, growing numbers of people who seek counseling and psychotherapy because of the discomfort of "a vital connection broken," or the "inability to communicate with those around," or psychic contactlessness despite "repeated attempts to reach out." All of these are causes and effects of the spiral of loneliness. The clinician observes, as did Fromm the analyst, Poe the poet, and Reissman the sociologist, that loneliness does not imply having no one around but does imply a feeling of being foreign in one's own space and the inability to "touch" another with one's own existence. This state of perceived contactlessness frequently creates a most desperate state of mind such that the experiencer cannot bear being alone. Like the old man in Poe's story, "The Man of the

Crowd,'' the desperately lonely person may restlessly follow groups or aggregates of people day and night, whenever he or she can find them without becoming a part of them. A look in any downtown bar in an American city at almost any hour of the day will reveal legions of such folk.

An example of such a person is a 29-year-old female client here named Jane who claims to have had difficulty communicating with her parents when she was very young. Shy in an elementary school that ''assisted in appropriate socialization,'' Jane isolated herself from other students and sought attention from her teacher by being obviously alone or frequently sick, eliciting both compassion and frequent talks. Jane tells her own story about the continued isolation of her adolescence and early adulthood.

> The closer I got to adolescence, the more intense the communication disorder became. As I entered puberty, I noticed that, like me, my peers began to be more aware of their physical appearance. As they began to gravitate toward developing intimate relationships with boys, and seeking popularity with each other, I developed a foreboding feeling—one of imminent disaster.
>
> Entering junior high school was truly devasting. I had been away with my family for the summer, and had missed orientation. When I went to school on day one, the size of the facility, and the increased number of other budding adolescents left me standing in a frozen position. When the bell rang, a friend of mine had to drag me into the building and explain the concept of ''homeroom.'' I remember shaking for hours that day. I entered a classroom with several others whom I had never laid eyes on before, and suddenly realized that I was in a situation where I had to ''talk'' to people I did not know. Finally, a couple of people I knew from elementary school entered the room, and the anxiety eased a little. At least I could talk to somebody, though it was not something I truly looked forward to doing. Therefore, seventh grade was not a particularly exciting experience.
>
> Eighth grade was different. Still seeking comfort in solitude, and communicating with others socially as little as possible, communication took a different turn. I began to take on the personality of the class clown. My grades were high, I was a teacher's pet in many instances because I always had my homework done and it was generally correct (with the exception of math, which was my worst subject). So, acting out without having to direct my conversation to any one particular individual, I learned to generalize to get attention.
>
> This was my way of gaining notoriety, while at the same time getting the attention I sought: one-to-one with my teachers. This was safe communication. It was a different kind of solitary that allowed

me to feel comfort in knowing that most of my teachers would not judge me or ridicule me for my looks, my smarts, etc., and hopefully they would understand me. I did not feel very understood by my parents, who found solace in sending me to a shrink and allowed me to maintain an inability to effectively socialize, and spent a great deal of time forbidding me to partake in the types of social activities that adolescents do. Therefore, I looked for solace of my own through other adult figures. This was how I avoided the rejection of my parents and peers. It was also, at this time, that I was becoming increasingly aware of my homosexuality. Additionally, the one person with whom I felt the closest, my father's mother, left to live in California because my mother disliked her living with us. I felt abandoned and more alone than before.

By ninth grade I was not only notorious in behavior, but I was now experiencing rejection from teachers. It was rejection in the sense that they would put a damper on my humorous nature, and instead of talking candidly and positively with me, they were enforcing punishment. This was a déjà vu of elementary school on a more sophisticated level. I created this situation for a particular reason: I was now more aware of my homosexual tendencies and my outward appearance was indicative of it, too. Therefore, I wanted control of the rejection by creating it myself in a way that was safe and gave me a reason to withdraw again. I was about to replace the hallowed halls of junior high school for those of senior high school.

My entry to high school was identical to that of junior high school. I had missed orientation, and now there were very few of my classmates that I had managed to send into hysterical laughter going with me, and I was about to face the most terrifying experience of my life. Peers were more cruel than before: They made frequent verbal comment as to my appearance (very masculine), and made direct statements that I was "queer." Again, I retreated to long periods of solitary, infrequent verbalizations (even in class), and seeking one-on-one attention from teachers when the need arose.

This was just the beginning of my loneliest period. I had no intimate relationships (only a couple of homosexual experimental situations that lasted a very short time). I was overweight, and basically unattractive. I had only one friend upon whom I leached whenever I could, and made no attempts to make any new friends. I was scared to death and contemplated suicide many times. I was arguing ferociously with my parents to allow me to get out of therapy, and spent long hours expressing my hatred of them for not allowing me to experience more independence than they considered feasible, as well as for sending my grandmother away, and began to spend a great deal of time contemplating defiant acts. The loneliness, to which I had become so attached, seemed to possess me to the point where I acted in ways to insure its permanence, blaming it on others, yet finding comfort in it as a way of life. This was to continue into my college years where the typical pathological behaviors of drinking and drug abuse entered the mainstream.

Growing up in a social environment that looked down on homosexuality, and when the topic of discussion of it was negative, to reveal the issue with my family was a constant source of anxiety. It was also a major influence on to the maintenance of my loneliness.

With respect to my family it was easy to slough off as "I am not seeing anyone right now because my school work is too important." This, of course, was perfectly acceptable to my family. However, to explain my single existence with no apparent interest in the opposite sex became difficult. Though later I would find out that my heterosexual friends knew all along and did not find it to be a reason to reject me, at the time I did not see it that way. Secretly, I engaged in homosexual relationships without any depth over the years I spent in college. Yet, I never established that intimate relationship which I sought. There was no one who could fill the void.

I began to rely heavily on my friends for attention, fun, and games. When their intimate relations would come to visit and distract my friends from paying attention to me, I became extemely jealous and experienced angry outbursts that communicated one thing, but not what it was that I was really feeling. I had lost touch with who I was, my feelings, my behavior, my wants, my desires. It was almost as though I established a schizophrenic existence which was negative and positive and not understood by anyone, including me. I was angry because I did not have what they had, and because I knew what to do about the situation but did not know how to go about it. I was afraid of the rejection that might ensue if my friends knew I was homosexual, and was lost in my own loneliness. I escaped through increased alcohol and drug abuse, and became so engaged with myself being defined through my livelihood as a teacher, that when I was laid off from work, I had more opportunity to get lost in the loneliness. I even became involved in heterosexual experiences and, to hide my homosexuality, got pregnant and had an abortion.

The pattern of Jane's downward-spiraling loneliness is apparent. Her early isolation from parents resulted in further isolation from peers. Ill equipped for social intercourse as an adolescent, she panicked and withdrew further into herself. Because her isolation was so painful, she masked herself and entered the crowd as a clown. From that time on her experiences with people were superficial, leading to ever increasing loneliness. Every attempted coping response, from her homosexuality to her attempts to deny it by means of an aborted pregnancy, made her feel more isolated in a crowd. For Jane, the eventual cure for loneliness was effective psychotherapy which led her from loneliness to solitude. She writes:

Getting caught up in one's loneliness is very easy. Refusing to confront the issue, the lonely person spends insurmountable hours feeling sorry for him/herself until they reach a level of depression that can, at times, be similar to that of manic-depression. This is an incredibly painful impact on the individual. One gets so caught up in oneself, that one is unable to acknowledge the existence of other persons and their feelings toward a situation. All that is perceived is one's own immediate condition and wallowing in it.

I "seriously" entered counseling and therapy. I say seriously here, because for approximately one year previous to this change I had been drinking heavily, missing appointments, arriving late to appointments, and dealing with it on my terms. I was eventually confronted on this issue, and it was a matter for me to consider: Do I, or don't I continue with counseling. I continued.

I took an apartment alone. At first, I was very uncomfortable there, but the more time I spent in the apartment the more I got in touch with my environment and with myself. I stopped running. I became depressed, but it was during these periods of depression that I came in touch with my feelings. Through therapy, I learned to identify my feelings and associate them with something. Many of my feelings were hostile. I became angry at what I considered to be distant, yet demanding parents. I directed both my hostility and my need for affection toward my therapist. It was also during these times that confrontation with loneliness became most difficult. The difficulty with confrontation was that I was creating my own condition and was unable to understand that I was responsbile for it, and I spent a great deal of time feeling misunderstood. In time, by working through my primary relationship with my therapist and obtaining meaningful work, I began to take off my mask. Loneliness masks the individual from facing his or her reality. When I began to see my own reality, I became able to touch others.

Jane's story is included here because it is a particularly lucid self-report of a person's journey through a depth of loneliness that to the experiencer seems almost impenetrable. To the therapist, however, the story is a common one. Loneliness was initially caused by an early-onset poverty in object relations resulting in a primarily intrapsychic disturbance. Furthermore, the disturbance was overcome in a relatively standard manner in that Jane, through therapy, found love within herself. Then, by finding meaningful work she became able to reach out to the world and find a measure of freedom.

Not all cases of loneliness, however, are primarily due to intrapsychic causes related to early deprivation in object relations. To assist the therapist in his or her understanding of the problem, Sadler (1974, 1978) speaks of five dimensions of the problem. Defining loneliness as feelings of apartness or separation, Sadler identifies psychological loneliness as feelings of being out of touch with parts of self. Interpersonal loneliness is the perception of self as separate from another. Social loneliness consists of a feeling of being ostracized or apart from the group. Cultural loneliness is defined as feelings of separation from others resulting from lack of culture or cultural change. Cosmic loneliness relates to feelings of separation from God or nature, or alienation from either because of spiritual severance.

The response to any of these dimensions of loneliness can be positive or negative. If positive, the loneliness is expressed as positive change in lifestyle or creativity. If negative, the response to loneliness on any dimension may be expressed as emptiness (a void with no one to fill it); hopelessness, isolation, and alienation, which carry the character of rejection; and ultimately, fear and anxiety.

Folkman and Lazarus (1980) contend that coping with loneliness may be problem focused or emotion focused. A problem-focused approach to the stress of loneliness involves changing interpersonal relationships or styles. An emotion-focused approach deals with managing the emotional stress that accompanies loneliness. All anxiety-management techniques from deep muscle relaxation to venting emotions apply to an emotion-focused stress-reduction procedure.

We contend that while both of these treatments, alone or in combination, are effective, they are maximized by helping clients to identify and cognitively map the causes and consequences of whatever dimension or dimensions of loneliness they are experiencing. To assist in this endeavor we have created what are simply called the five C's. Cosmic loneliness estranges us from communion, cultural loneliness from custom, social loneliness from community, interpersonal loneliness from companionship, and psychological or intrapsychic loneliness from congruence.

Once the loneliness is identified (this is essential to minimize generalization) the client can then personalize it through telling his or her own story in much the manner of Jane. The client also needs time to be in solitude with his or her awareness of the new pinpointed condition. In the solitude a journal is in order where grief over one's emerging explicit condition can be expressed, where recurrent patterns can be iterated and explored, and where the negative feelings of anxiety and loss can be creatively expressed. Sadler (1978) contends that there are four sequential stages of loneliness that can be sorted out with ease: (1) a causal event or events; (2) the experience itself; (3) the consequences of the experience; (4) the coping responses effected by the experience. Each of the five dimensions of loneliness with its concomitant special loss can be viewed by client and therapist in each of its four stages. The following cases illustrate this concept.

Mark T. was basically a spiritual person. Poet, artist, and teacher, Mark earned a living as an English professor in a community college. His work, he felt, was his mission. Mark was dedicated to his family as well as to his career. When his twin sons reached adolescence, Mark, then 38 years of age, became acutely aware that his income was limited. He wanted to provide his children a college education, so when he was afforded an opportunity to increase his income by entering administration as assistant dean of instruction, he did so. For the next 10 years he worked very hard, was promoted to dean, and finally to president.

At the age of 48 Mark had both sons in their junior year of college, rarely saw them or his wife, worked long hours, no longer painted or wrote poetry, and showed the scars of many budget battles, political victories and a few defeats. Whereas he once had a sense of mission about his teaching, he now had none about his presidency. He tried to pray and could not find his god. Whereas he once enjoyed fishing with his young sons, he no longer enjoyed nature. He worked like a machine and felt disconnected from the universe that once nurtured him. The more he worked, the more alienated he felt, the more he worked. Once he enjoyed the fellowship of peers; now there were those people that he used and those who used him.

Mark and his wife attended social events frequently. They always looked good; their private conversation was of the family budget, their growing sons, and the next event.

At the end of Mark's 49th year, his 74-year-old father suffered a stroke which he miraculously survived. During his father's illness, Mark wanted to cry out to God but could not. He wanted the companionship of his wife and sons but did not know how to reach them. He could no longer lose himself in work. Often at night he would enter his study and stare into space. One night he sat there in terror. Hours later, with tears streaming down his face, Mark went to bed. He slept only fitfully. The next day he entered therapy.

Though Mark's cosmic loneliness effected his social life and his intrapsychic processes, he was primarily estranged from communion. As a youth he communed with nature, God, and his own core. It took his father's brush with death to cause Mark to become consciously aware of the aridity of his own life, an aridity that was initially caused when he left his mission to teach and became an administrator. Once set on what was for him a lonely course, he experienced even greater alienation from his spiritual core. Consequently, he became more and more a highly skilled automaton who coped with his cosmic aloneness by increasing his work load. The downward spiral was set.

Part of Mark's therapy involved solitude. He remained college president but, once aware of *how* he was doing his job, he became a participant observer and distanced himself. He was also told to write an autobiography, a little bit each day. At first, his words were stilted but before long his creativity returned. He remembered that when he was a youth his father taught him how important it was to support a family. Income equaled success in Mark's version of Dad's eyes. He had rebelled somewhat, wanted to be a free spirit . . . wanted to become a teacher . . . became one.

Mark then understood the deeper causes of his loneliness and one day he forgave himself. When he could again commune with himself, then he could again pray, again write and fish. The skills that he had learned during the sterile years did not leave him. He could be a college president and live and laugh and teach.

Mark's cosmic loneliness had a precipitating cause and an underlying one. His experience and its consequences could be traced along his attempted coping mechanisms.

Like Mark, Sheila B. was also able to gain insight into the process of her loneliness. Born a Jewess, Sheila enjoyed the foods of Passover, the tradition of Rosh Hashanah and Yom Kippur, the celebration of Succoth and the closeness of the suburban "ghetto" that grew up around the neighborhood market, the cleaners, the synagogue, and the local movie house. Sheila was the oldest of four children. The others were boys whose ages dropped in two-year steps behind her own.

Sheila's family was not wealthy but it was close on her mother's side. Dad was an itinerant and somewhat errant yard-goods salesman. To Sheila, Mom was the backbone of the universe.

When Sheila was 16 years old her mother died. Sheila quit school, went to work, and kept house for her brothers. Mother's family helped; Dad was less and less around. At the age of 18 Sheila met and fell in love with Sean, an Irish Catholic, who had a steady job. They married, at which time Sheila was disowned by her family. Mother's relatives cared for Sheila's brothers, and Dad and his family disappeared. Sheila kept contact with her brothers but she was no longer invited to Seders and was shunned by the members of the synagogue.

Sean was good to Sheila, as was his family who took her in, but she longed for the customs of her childhood. She missed the "ghetto" and she frequently took buses through it "just to look." She never got off the bus; she felt unwelcome, yet she continued to ride several days a week for several years.

Sean's family adored her. When she had few coins to take her bus trips, they gave her some. They also introduced her to their pastor and welcomed her to their church. She went, but she felt a stranger.

When Sheila was 21 years old and Sean was 23 years old they had a child. Sheila wanted her daughter to have a religion. She had her daughter baptized a Catholic. Four years later Sheila and Sean had a second daughter who was also baptized Catholic.

Sean never pressured Sheila to become a Catholic and Sheila never stopped her bus trips through the old neighborhood. One day her youngest brother, like the two older boys, left the nest and joined the armed services. That day, very quietly, Sheila joined the church of her children and husband. From then on new customs replaced the old ones that she never forgot. Her brothers, when they returned from the service, married. They did not follow their father's ways for they and their families loved Sheila. To them she was Catholic, not dead. Once again, Sheila was invited to Seders, and she, with Sean, went to them. However, she now identified with her new family and the customs of her new faith.

Obviously, the cause of Sheila's cultural loneliness was the disowning of her by her family of origin when she married a man not of her faith. This cultural loneliness with its consequential void of familiar customs followed closely on the grief reaction Sheila experienced at the death of her mother.

Not ready to divorce herself from her past, though viewed as dead to her orthodox Jewish relatives, Sheila coped with her loneliness by her seemingly endless bus rides. Through the glass windows of the bus she stared at a cultural environment that she could not touch. Ultimately, she replaced her old environment with a new one, her old customs with new ones. She then connected as closely with Christians as she once had connected with Jews.

Cultural loneliness is commonly alleviated when new customs are acquired. The acquisition of new customs, however, is not easy, particularly when they are ego-alien. Refugees who experience cultural loneliness frequently face adapting to cultures far different from their own. On the other hand it is not uncommon, once new customs are acquired, for people to discard the old, never to return to them.

Lynwood M. worked for the Gas and Electric Company for 41 years. During those years he worked his way up from billing clerk to middle management. He was loyal worker, a company man, and he never missed the annual picnic. His friends were his co-workers with whom he carpooled during the week and played horseshoes on weekends. Of the group of co-workers, Lynwood was the oldest.

When Lynwood was 65 they retired him—dinner, imitation gold watch, and everything. Retirement separated Lynwood not only from work but from a community of friends who shared a common life. Lynwood had always said that he wanted to travel when he retired, but instead he stayed at home. He wore work clothes instead of suits, but he did not work around the house. Some days he didn't even shave. Lynwood's social loneliness, caused by retirement, separated Lynwood from his community. The feeling was that of being cast out, abandoned, ostracized. In shock, despite the fact he knew retirement to be imminent, Lynwood's response was depression.

For Lynwood, the first step toward healing is recognition of where he is and what retirement has done to him by divorcing him from the community. Healing will come only when he can find a new community and a place for himself within it. Lynwood is legion!

Death and divorce are common causes of interpersonal loneliness. The experience is generally one of longing for lost companionship. In mourners the longing is usually person specific; in divorce, generalized. Margo was divorced after being married for 17 years. In addition to the loss of the companionship of a mate, she knew that much of her loneliness was social. She could no longer travel as couple with coupled friends. When the group went to the symphony in pairs, Margo joined them alone a few times, then dropped out.

For Margo, marriage had been sour for some time. She suffered the effects of interpersonal loneliness then too, because Jim wasn't really there for her. There was no warmth or caring coming from him. Socially they had been a couple but the close companionship was gone.

Margo needs help in tracing the causes of it all. She says over and over again, "I don't really know how or when it happened." Margo both saw and refused to see. Like Lynwood, Margo, too, is legion.

Loss of congruence is indicative of alienation from self and the experience of the inherent loneliness in this intrapsychic phenomenon. Mildred, aged 43, learned that she had Hodgkin's Disease, Stage III A. She received radiation treatments for several months and the disease supposedly entered remission, only to return 3 years later in her lungs. This time chemotherapy was ordered. Again, Mildred improved but the drugs, coupled with her distress over her illness and the necessity of chemotherapy, caused intense feelings of separation from self loneliness. At times it became difficult for Mildred to identify with her own body. At times she felt that out of touch with herself as though she were apart from herself. She experienced the incongruence most acutely at the time of her treatments.

The intensity of the feeling of loneliness is compounded when single dimensions combine, as they often do. Sheila's loneliness was primarily cultural, but also social in that she had been ostracized by her family of origin. Lynwood's loneliness was social but with strong intrapsychic components. Mark's cosmic loneliness had traces of all other dimensions within it; and Margo's loneliness, as was already demonstrated, had social as well as interpersonal components.

In summary, Sadler's (1974,1978) schema, which states that all loneliness can be broken into four stages from causal to experiential, to consequential, to coping resources crosses all five fundamental types. Furthermore, Sadler's five fundamental types of loneliness—cosmic, cultural, social, interpersonal and intrapsychic can be defined by their consequent losses. These losses, or deprivations, correspond to the fundamental types as loss of communion, custom, community, companionship, and congruence. Easily remembered as "the 5 C's," these losses clearly identify types of loneliness.

There is an enormous body of literature stating that what we can understand we can learn to control. Though there is much more to be learned about loneliness, Sadler afforded us a model that can be used for both research and practice. To work effectively with loneliness, therapists must simply give clients constructs which to define it. These aspects should also help clients by giving them activities such as writing songs, poems, or stories about their loneliness so that they can personalize it. The creativity involved in such activity helps one contact one's inner self and begin to create a positive response. Therapists also need to allow their clients the time and solitude that Jane and Mark allowed themselves. Positive solitude almost always invites presence, and a sense of presence dispels loneliness. Finally, therapists help clients find recurrent patterns or themes in their lives. Discovery of these enables clients to reach the core of their loneliness, the base of the spiral, and the beginning of the long trip back to congruence, companions, customs, community, and communion.

REFERENCES

Englehart, H.T. (1974). Solitude and sociality. *Humanitas*, *10*.
Folkman, S. & Lazarus, P.S. (1980). An analysis of coping in a middle-aged community sample. *Journal of Health and Social Behavior*, *21*.
Fromm-Reichmann, F. (1959). On loneliness. In D.M. Bullard (Ed.), *Psychoanalysis and psychotherapy, Selected papers of Frieda Fromm-Reichmann* (pp. 325-336). Chicago: University of Chicago Press.
Moustakas, C. (1961). *Loneliness*. Englewood Cliffs: Prentice-Hall.
Sadler, W.A. Jr. (1974). On the verge of a lonely life. *Humanitas*, *10*.
Sadler, W.A. Jr. (1978). Dimensions in the problem of loneliness: A phenomenological approach. *Journal of Phenomenological Psychology*, *9* (1-2).
Satran, G. (1978). Notes on loneliness, from a paper given at Grand Rounds, Roosevelt Hospital Department of Psychiatry, Novermber, 1975. *Journal of the American Academy of Psychoanalysis*, *6* (3).
Sobosan, J.G. (1978). Loneliness and faith. *Journal of Psychology and Theology*, *6* (2).
Sullivan, H.S. (1953). *The interpersonal theory of psychiatry*. New York: Norton.
Webster's New World Dictionary. (1978). Second College Edition, D.B. Guralnick, (Ed.). William Collins and World Publishing Co.
Weiss, R.S. (1973). *Loneliness: The experience of emotional and social isolation*, Cambridge, MA: MIT Press.